Presented to:

. . . .

From:

. . . .

Date:

. . . .

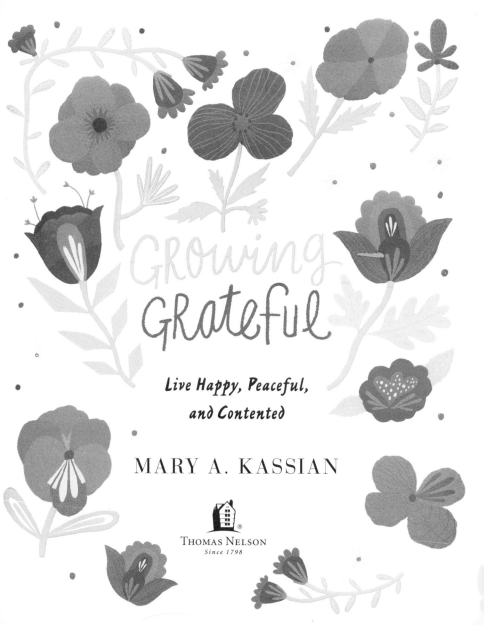

Growing Grateful

Live Happy, Peaceful, and Contented

MARY A. KASSIAN

THOMAS NELSON
Since 1798

Published in Nashville, Tennessee, by Thomas Nelson. Thomas Nelson is a registered trademark of HarperCollins Christian Publishing, Inc.

Published in association with the literary agency of Wolgemuth & Associates, Inc.

Cover art by Carolyn Gavin

Thomas Nelson titles may be purchased in bulk for educational, business, fund-raising, or sales promotional use. For information, please e-mail SpecialMarkets@ThomasNelson.com.

ISBN 978–1–4002–0938–5

Printed in Canada

20 21 22 23 24   FR   11 10 9 8 7 6 5 4 3

Contents

Let us be grateful.

Hebrews 12:28 ESV

grateful

grate·ful | \ ˈgrāt-fəl \
adjective

1. warmly or deeply appreciative of kindness or benefits received; thankful.

    [*I'm grateful for your help.*]

2. expressing or characterized by gratitude.

    [*a grateful glance*]

3. pleasing to the mind or senses; agreeable or welcome; refreshing.

    [*a grateful drink of water*]

Foreword

Hey friend, I'm so glad you picked up this book. I believe it contains the antidote for any anxiety, discontent, or frustration you may struggle with. When your gratefulness grows, your anxiety, discontent, and frustration will begin to shrink.

We all have areas or situations in our lives that don't make gratitude an easy attitude to have or choice to make, right? Illness. Loss. Rejection. Loneliness. Blindness.

Well, that last one is mine. I became blind as a fifteen-year-old girl because of a disease and now, decades later, I've lived in darkness longer than I ever lived in light. So I know how hard gratefulness can be. Sometimes life is just plain hard, and we don't feel grateful one bit. That's when gratitude is a sacrifice. It is a sacrifice we give to God, yet it is also a gift He gives to us.

The Lord says, "The one who offers thanksgiving as his sacrifice glorifies me; to one who orders his way rightly I will show the salvation of God!" (Psalm 50:23 ESV).

Did you notice in that verse that being grateful to God is a sacrifice—that it costs us something? It's not always easy. The verse tells us that if we want to live the right way ("order our way rightly"), then we need to do the hard and liberating work of growing in gratitude. Our gratitude shows off His goodness to a world that needs to see it. And when we grow in gratefulness, we grow closer to the Lord.

Honestly, if God hadn't helped me grow in gratefulness and given me the grace to offer Him my sacrifice of thanksgiving, I don't know how I would make it through one more day of blindness.

I don't want you to try to make it through one more day of anxiety, discontent, frustration—or whatever you're feeling—without the gift of gratitude supporting you. I want you to grow in gratefulness and grow closer to the Lord along with it.

My friend, as your gratefulness grows, so will your capacity to perceive blessings, even when they're shrouded in hardship. That's why I'm so thankful that my friend Mary wrote this book. She's filled every page with solid, biblical reasons for you to offer up gratitude to God. She'll help you grow grateful in ways that glorify Him and bless you. Linger with the questions for meditation found at the end of each entry. Make each topic of gratitude your focus for the day. Gratitude has made all the difference in my life. And it will in your life too. You will become more happy, peaceful, and contented as you grow more grateful. So cozy up and get started.

Love,
Jennifer Rothschild

1 · *So Good to Be Grateful*

It is good to give thanks to the LORD.
PSALM 92:1 ESV

Research reveals that being grateful comes with a crop of side benefits.[1] People who are grateful are more hopeful, energetic, and positive, while being less envious, anxious, and depressed. Grateful people also tend to have more willpower and be more empathetic, compassionate, and helpful—and to have greater integrity and faith. Overall they feel significantly more optimistic and satisfied with life than those who fail to express gratitude.

In her book *The How of Happiness: A New Approach to Getting the Life You Want*, professor Sonja Lyubomirsky concludes that gratitude is a kind of meta-strategy for achieving happiness. It's the virtue that opens the door to all sorts of other good habits and feelings.[2]

The fact that gratitude is the root of many other virtues would not come as a surprise to the psalmist in today's scripture. His expressions of thanks and praise were bountiful, so he undoubtedly experienced many of gratitude's benefits. He noted, "It is *good*"—that is, right and enjoyable—to give thanks. As we grow more grateful we'll see other beautiful things sprout up in our lives. As gratitude grows, our peace, contentment, and happiness will bloom too. Like the psalmist, we'll experience how very good it is to give thanks.

MEDITATION

Have you ever considered that gratitude is the parent of peace, contentment, and happiness? What do your levels of peace, contentment, and happiness indicate about your need to grow more grateful?

GROW GRATEFUL
Increase your happiness quotient by offering up some prayers of gratitude.

2 · *Growing Grateful*

> As the earth brings forth its sprouts, and as a garden causes what is sown in it to sprout up, so the Lord GOD will cause righteousness and praise to sprout up before all the nations.
> ISAIAH 61:11 ESV

In my part of the world, winter lingers until the end of March or even longer. By then I'm tired of the cold, white, lifeless landscape. I yearn for the prairie crocus. This member of the buttercup family is the first flower to burst through the snow and defy the monochromatic scenery. With vivid purple, yellow, and green, it heralds the coming of spring.

I'm always elated to spot the first crocus. Because I know that the daffodils and tulips will rush to follow its lead. The trees will soon blush green. Lilacs, apple blossoms, and lilies of the valley will perfume the air. I'll plant sweet pea seeds and vegetable seedlings in my garden. Fill the massive clay pot on my deck with herbs. Bed geraniums, petunias, and begonias in the raised planter encircling my patio. Over the course of the summer, I'll watch the blooms multiply and spill over the stone walls. I'll pick fragrant herbs for my recipes. Harvest tasty fruit and vegetables for my table. And delight in the beauty and wonder of it all.

Scripture indicates that the Lord causes goodness and gratitude to sprout up in our hearts like shoots in a garden. Gratitude is just as important to Him as goodness. The Gardener of our hearts doesn't only want us to grow more holy; He also wants us to grow more grateful. He longs to see gratefulness spring up in your life even more than northerners long for the first flowers of spring.

MEDITATION

Is your heart's garden blooming with gratitude? Would you characterize it as being in a state of winter or spring? What do you think you can do to grow more grateful?

GROW GRATEFUL
Pray and ask the Lord to help you grow more grateful.

3 · *Grateful to You, God*

> I thank God through Jesus Christ our Lord!
> Romans 7:25

A few weeks ago I watched a reality show starring an organizational guru who helps people declutter their homes. She had a lot of good tips for organizing things, but one part of her intervention puzzled me. Prior to getting started, she had the homeowners kneel in the room and give thanks. Then she had them hug each piece of outdated clothing or junk they were about to trash or recycle, and give thanks for that too.

I was confused. The "you" in her "thank-you" had no object. She didn't explain to whom the thanks ought to be directed. Am I supposed to thank my old blouse? The factory that stitched it? The friend who gifted it to me? The spirit of my closet? The decluttering gods?

True gratitude—Christian gratitude—doesn't exist in a vacuum. It's more than a warm, fuzzy feeling of appreciation for something good that comes my way. It's far deeper and more profound than that.

It rises above every other form of gratitude, for it acknowledges that God, the Father of Jesus Christ, is the ultimate source of all blessing. True gratitude recognizes that "there is one God, the Father. All things are from Him" and that "there is one Lord, Jesus Christ. All things are through Him" (1 Corinthians 8:6).

A heart that is grateful—but not grateful to God—isn't grateful in the right sort of way. True gratitude recognizes that God is the "You" we must thank.

MEDITATION

Are you grateful to God, or are you merely grateful? Do you recognize that all the blessings that come your way ultimately come from God through Jesus Christ?

GROW GRATEFUL
Tell God what blessings you are grateful for today.

4 · *Grateful for Good Things from Above*

Every generous act and every perfect gift is from
above, coming down from the Father of lights.
JAMES 1:17

"Surprise!" hollered the group of people hiding in my kitchen. I *was*
surprised! My birthday had passed, and I thought the celebrations
were over. My granddaughters giggled with excitement as they gave
me a tour of their bubblegum-pink, princess-themed decorations and
cake. I could tell from the care given to detail and the quality of the
spread on the table that my two daughters-in-law had played a major
role in putting the party together.

After the guests left I gave my daughters-in-law big hugs and
thanked them. *"That's* who you should thank," quipped Jacqueline,
pointing to my husband, who was sitting on the counter grinning like
the cat who'd just swallowed the canary. *"He* instigated it all!"

Of course I thanked him too.

Today's scripture tells us that *every* generous act and *every* perfect gift comes from God. Even when we receive good things from other people, God is ultimately the instigator behind the gifts. The apostle Paul understood this. He didn't just thank his friends for their friendship; he *thanked God* for them (Philippians 1:3). He didn't just thank Titus for his concern; he *thanked God* for stirring up this feeling in Titus's heart (2 Corinthians 8:16). He didn't just thank the Corinthians for their generosity; he *thanked God* for granting them the capacity and desire to give (2 Corinthians 9:11).

Paul thanked his friends. But he recognized that God had a part in their kindness and generosity. So he thanked God too.

MEDITATION

When people do nice things for you or give you a gift, do you thank God too? If you understood that God was the mastermind behind all these kindnesses, how would that impact your view of Him?

GROW GRATEFUL

Express thanks to someone today. And don't forget to thank God for that person too.

5 · *Grateful with Praise and Thanksgiving*

> Acknowledge that Yahweh is God. . . . Enter His
> gates with thanksgiving and His courts with praise.
> Give thanks to Him and praise His name.
> PSALM 100:3–4

Did you know that there are more than two thousand verses in the Bible that encourage us to be grateful? They exhort us to "Praise the Lord!" "Give thanks to the Lord!" and "Bless the Lord!" Praise focuses on God's character and nature. It expresses awe and gratitude for *who He is*. Giving thanks focuses on God's gifts and other benefits we receive from Him. It expresses gratitude for *what He does*. To *bless* God is to praise and thank Him with reverence.

Christian gratitude takes the spotlight off *self* and shines it on God. Rather than simply being thankful for something we have received, our hearts overflow with praise and thanksgiving for everything *He* is and everything *He* does. This forces us to move beyond adoring the gift to adoring the Giver.

Are you as surprised as I was to find out how many times the Bible encourages us to be grateful? Thousands! The number is staggering. It's far more than the number of times we're encouraged to pray or to forgive. I think it's fair to conclude from these frequent exhortations that gratitude is not an incidental, secondary virtue in the Christian life. It's of primary importance. Godly people are grateful people. And they're grateful, above all, with praise and thanks to God.

MEDITATION

Why do you think the Bible places such emphasis on being grateful to God? How does gratitude take the spotlight off *self* and shine it on Him? Which character traits of God are you the most grateful for?

GROW GRATEFUL
Spend some time praising God for who He is and what He does.

6 · *Choose to Be Grateful*

> My soul, praise the LORD, and do
> not forget all His benefits.
> PSALM 103:2

Listening to the radio one day, I heard something so profound that I ran for a pen and sticky note to write it down. Author Elisabeth Elliot said, "It is always possible to be thankful for what is given rather than to complain about what is not given—one or the other becomes a habit of life."[3]

I felt convicted. I was a young mom at home with a new baby. I had been feeling sorry for myself and whining about what I lacked (sleep, mostly). The negativity was becoming a habit. "I choose to be grateful," I whispered as I fastened the sticky note to a prominent place above my desk.

I recited the quote often—as I tended to my fussy baby, performed menial household chores, and washed yet another load of soiled diapers. (Yes, washed! The eco movement had shamed me into using cloth.) Like David in today's scripture, I counseled my soul not to forget the many ways God had blessed me. The quote became a mantra of sorts. I hung the note in various places in my house until the ink faded.

Years later, I met Elisabeth Elliot in person. Excitedly, I told her how deeply that quote had impacted me. "Did I say that?" she laughed, and then paused. Perhaps she was thinking of her murdered husband, or of the second husband she had lost to cancer. "Yes, indeed," she affirmed, squeezing my hand and giving me a big smile. "It *is* always possible to be thankful!"

MEDITATION

Are you thankful for what is given or are you complaining about what you didn't get? Which attitude is becoming a habit of life for you?

GROW GRATEFUL
In prayer, commit to be someone
who chooses to be grateful.

7 · *Grateful Is Beautiful*

Rejoice in the LORD, you righteous ones;
praise from the upright is beautiful.
PSALM 33:1

When I worked as a therapist at a rehabilitation hospital, I observed a stark difference in the attitudes of two of my elderly patients. One was a below-knee amputee who had been fitted with a prosthesis. The other had an archive of debilitating ailments that rivaled the number of items on a holiday grocery shopping list. Yet the lady with the debilitating physical condition was cheerful and grateful, while the amputee was an intolerable grump. Their rooms were next to one another, which made the contrast between the two women even more striking.

The drapes in the cheerful woman's room were open to let in the light. Nurses and therapists loved to meet this woman's needs, for they were always greeted with a pleasant smile, laughter, and an appreciative "Thank you so much, dear!" The grumpy woman kept her drapes drawn. She wallowed in darkness. Instead of laughter, one could often hear loud, critical complaints and verbal assaults as she castigated yet another health-care worker. "Thanks" wasn't in her vocabulary. I dreaded going into her room.

Gratitude is far more attractive than ingratitude. Grateful people are just such lovely people to be around. Psalm 33:1 reinforces that a cheerful, thankful demeanor is "beautiful." Another translation puts it this way: "praise *befits* the upright" (ESV, emphasis added). In other words, not only is gratitude admirable, it's the proper and right attitude for God's people to adopt. Make a point of expressing gratitude today. Regardless of your circumstances, the Lord wants you to exude more of this beautiful, endearing trait.

MEDITATION

Would the people in your family describe you as a grateful person or as a grumpy person? Do you think a grateful person is more attractive than a grumpy one? Why?

GROW GRATEFUL
Ask the Lord to help you cultivate a cheerful, thankful demeanor.

8 · *Grateful Words*

> I will fervently thank the LORD with my mouth;
> I will praise Him in the presence of many.
> PSALM 109:30

My granddaughter Callie is just learning how to talk. She has about a dozen words in her vocabulary, including *mama, dada, bye-bye,* and *na-na* (banana). She's also starting to say *peese* (please) and *dat-doo* (thank you). Her parents prompt her to say *please* each time she reaches out for something she wants and *thank you* after she receives it. It makes me smile when I drop a handful of cereal on the tray of her high chair and she spontaneously responds with an exuberant "Dat-doo!"

Her parents aren't just training Callie to be polite. They're helping her to develop an attitude of gratitude *and* to avoid an attitude of entitlement. Although hearing her say "please" and "thank you" brings them joy, the words are for her benefit more than theirs. It's vital that she learns to *express* gratitude so that an attitude of gratitude might sprout up in her heart.

Notice in today's verse that David fervently thanked the Lord with his mouth. His gratitude wasn't silent. He gave thanks to God out loud so others could hear. This practice undeniably had a boomerang effect, transforming him into a more grateful person. The importance of expressing gratitude verbally—out loud with words—can't be overstated. There's a strong connection between our words and our attitudes, so strong that changing one usually changes the other. I'll let you in on a secret: the best way to grow grateful in your heart is to become increasingly grateful with your words, saying "thank you" out loud.

MEDITATION

Do you make a habit of expressing gratitude out loud? What kind of impact do you think this practice might have in your life? How about in the lives of the people who hear your words of gratitude?

GROW GRATEFUL
Express your gratitude to God and
to others out loud today.

9 • *Called to Be Grateful*

> Give thanks in everything, for this is
> God's will for you in Christ Jesus.
>
> 1 THESSALONIANS 5:18

Gratitude is a popular concept these days. Amazon lists thousands of items that capitalize on the trend: gratitude books, gratitude journals, gratitude calendars, gratitude wall decor, gratitude mugs and bracelets. Even gratitude socks! These items appeal to the masses because all of us yearn to experience greater happiness, peace, and contentment. And most of us have heard that growing grateful is the key.

God calls us to be grateful. It's His will for us in Christ Jesus. And Christian gratitude has a far different texture to it than the type of gratitude promoted in shopping malls. Biblical gratitude is more than baubles engraved with inspirational mottos. It's more than remembering to be polite and say "thank you" when folks do something nice. It's more than journaling three grateful thoughts a day. It's more than shoring up our feelings through self-help methods.

The Bible indicates that gratitude is a Spirit-filled discipline. It's the process through which we habitually recognize God's greatness and acknowledge Him as the One from whom all blessings flow. As my friend Nancy says, "Gratitude is a lifestyle. A *hard-fought*, grace-infused, *biblical lifestyle.*"

In a general sense, we can all benefit from growing more grateful. Even those who haven't put their faith in Jesus can benefit. But there's another sense in which unbelievers don't—indeed can't—grasp what gratitude truly means. Because they don't have a relationship with the Source of everything good, they miss out on being grateful in the right kind of way.

MEDITATION

Why is gratitude a spiritual discipline and a biblical lifestyle for Christians? How does this differ from the type of gratitude sold to the masses? How can you practice gratitude as a Spirit-filled discipline?

GROW GRATEFUL
Pray for more discipline to practice gratitude as a lifestyle.

10 · *Careful to Grow Grateful*

> Though they knew God, they did not glorify Him as
> God or show gratitude. Instead, their thinking became
> nonsense, and their senseless minds were darkened.
> ROMANS 1:21

My brothers and I once got a huge set of dominoes for Christmas. We
learned to match the pips (dots) on the bones (tiles) to play games of
Block Dominoes and Train Dominoes. But more than playing those
games, I enjoyed placing all the bones on end on the floor one after
another in a long row. After painstakingly setting them up, I was ready
for the big moment. I tipped the first one over to initiate the chain
reaction. Then I watched in fascination as they clicked and toppled in
sequence all the way across the room.

We've already discussed the fact that gratitude produces greater
happiness, peace, contentment, and other positive virtues and benefits. But have you ever stopped to consider that the opposite is equally
true? Just as gratitude produces a domino effect of good in our lives, so

ingratitude produces a domino effect of harm. Today's verse illustrates this clearly. Failing to be grateful comes with terrible consequences. Our thinking become nonsense. Our minds become darkened. In other words, ingratitude negatively affects our reasoning and our perception.

People who are ungrateful are more envious, anxious, and depressed, and less hopeful, energetic, and agreeable. Ungrateful people also tend to be more apathetic, insensitive, callous, and nasty—and to have less integrity and faith.[4] Ingratitude produces a crop of ugly, destructive weeds that choke out the goodness and beauty in our lives.

The warning is sobering. Growing grateful isn't just beneficial—it's actually *crucial* to our well-being.

MEDITATION

Do you feel as if there's an absence of goodness and beauty in your life? Is it possible that ingratitude is choking them out? What can you do today to get rid of this destructive weed?

GROW GRATEFUL
Express gratitude to someone you
have recently criticized.

11 · *Grateful That God Is Good*

You are good, and You do what is good.
PSALM 119:68

Greek mythology contains a large collection of stories about the lives and adventures of dozens of gods and goddesses. These pseudodeities each had unique realms of influence. Like Gaia, the mother earth goddess. Zeus, the god of the sky. Poseidon, the god of the sea. Or Athena, the goddess of wisdom, skill, and war. Yet despite their immortality and superhero-like abilities, all of them were plagued with destructive emotions and severe character flaws. They were powerful—but they were not completely *good*.

Can you imagine what it would be like to serve a deity who was arrogant, abusive, immoral, fickle, treacherous, or vindictive? Or one who was immature, impatient, inconsistent, or prone to fly off the handle in an uncontrolled rage? I am so glad our God is not like that. Scripture is clear that He doesn't have any character flaws. No. The Lord is altogether *good*.

When Moses boldly asked God to reveal Himself, do you know what God showed him? He showed Moses His *goodness* (Exodus 33:19–20). Moses caught only a fleeting glimpse. But God's goodness was so perfect, so wonderful, and so spectacular that even this brief exposure caused the skin on Moses' face to glow.

God is the very definition of good. He doesn't merely do good things. He *is* good. His character is morally excellent and extraordinarily beautiful. The psalmist encourages us to test this fact out for ourselves: "Taste and see that the LORD is good. How happy is the man who takes refuge in Him" (Psalm 34:8).

MEDITATION

How can we be grateful for God's goodness even when our circumstances aren't good? How would an appreciation for God's goodness make a difference in how we handle the difficulty?

GROW GRATEFUL
Thank the Lord for His extraordinary goodness.

12 · *Grateful That God Is Great*

> My soul, praise Yahweh! LORD my God,
> You are very great; You are clothed
> with majesty and splendor.
> PSALM 104:1

First-time visitors to the Grand Canyon in northwest Arizona are usually so awestruck by the sight that they stand gawking in stunned silence. The feature that makes this gorge the most spectacular of all the seven natural wonders of the world is its immense size. Some visitors hover above it in a helicopter to get a better sense of its dimensions. But it's still hard to grasp. The canyon is so vast and deep that it fills your entire field of vision. And the more you stare, the harder it becomes to retain a sense of proportion. One travelers' guide to the Grand Canyon says that "distance becomes meaningless, depth blurs, and your sense of time and space withers away."[5]

People are overwhelmed by how teeny and microscopic they feel standing in the presence of something so grand and magnificent. The psalmist who penned today's verse felt the same way. He exclaimed, "LORD my God, You are *very great*."

We can't even begin to fathom the greatness—that is, the immensity, the magnitude, and the magnificence—of God. The Grand Canyon and every other natural wonder are teeny and microscopic by comparison. God is greater. His greatness eclipses His creation. Everything about Him is great. His goodness is great. His power is great. His love is great. Job exclaimed, "How great is God—beyond our understanding!" (Job 36:26 NIV).

Oh, that we might take the time to gawk in wonder.

MEDITATION

Have you ever been awestruck by the greatness of a mountain, canyon, or other natural wonder? Think about the fact that God is greater. Does this fill you with wonder and awe?

GROW GRATEFUL
Take some time—in prayer—to gawk in wonder at the greatness of God.

13 · *Grateful That God Is All-Powerful*

> Yours, LORD, is the greatness and the power and
> the glory and the splendor and the majesty. . . .
> Power and might are in Your hand, and it is in Your
> hand to make great and to give strength to all.
> 1 CHRONICLES 29:11–12

Marvel comics and movies recount the fictional adventures of ordinary people who've been imbued with superpowers. One of their most hyped movies features the story of Carol Danvers, an air force pilot. An explosion of an alien substance transforms her into Captain Marvel—one of the universe's most powerful superheroes. This mega superwoman runs at six times the speed of sound, possesses superhuman strength and durability, shoots concussive energy bursts from her fingertips, and can vanquish every foe.

Outside of the movie theater we know that humans can't make

bullets bounce off their chests, or run faster than a train, or fly, or leap over tall buildings in a single bound. Humans are just so . . . human! Still, we like to think we have power and control over our lives. All it takes is a sudden change in circumstance—an illness, an accident, a natural disaster, a financial or relational loss—to confront us with the reality that we don't.

God is the only true Superpower. All power belongs to Him. His ability is unrestricted. God's power is greater than the power of an earthquake. It is greater than the sun's most radiant beam and the sky's most ferocious bolt of lightning. His power is greater than every government, every army, every boss, every relative, every friend. It is greater than every disaster, every hardship, every challenge, and every heartbreak. His power can accomplish abundantly more than you could ask, think, or ever imagine. And He makes this power available to you.

MEDITATION

Have you ever felt weak and lacking in power? How does it make you feel that God extends His great power to you and gives you strength? In what area of your life do you need more of His power?

• • • • •

GROW GRATEFUL
Praise the Lord for His great power and might.

14 · *Grateful That God Reigns*

> He is the blessed and only Sovereign, the
> King of kings, and the Lord of lords.
> 1 TIMOTHY 6:15

Have you ever been in a castle? I actually lived in one! After high school I attended a Bible school that was housed in a nineteenth-century castle set on rolling acres of park land near England's famous Lake District. My dorm came complete with stone walls, towering arched windows, spiraling staircases, balustrades, and turrets. I also trekked through Europe visiting other castles, like the opulent Chateau de Versailles, home of King Louis XIV, the great monarch of France.

The word *monarch* drives from the Greek *monos archein*, meaning "one ruler." A monarchy is a form of government in which the right to rule is passed down from one generation to the next. Once crowned, a king or queen rules for life. Although modern monarchs are often figureheads with little power, historically their power was absolute. If the monarch ruled an independent territory, he or she was its sovereign—supreme in power, free of outside influence and control.

The Bible teaches that God is sovereign. He is supreme—far above all rule and authority, power and dominion, and every title that can be given (Ephesians 1:21). He reigns. He is in control. No matter what happens in our political, economic, or social structures. No matter what happens in our professional or personal lives. No matter what happens with our finances, our health, or our relationships. No matter what kind of havoc and destruction comes our way. We can be certain and grateful that heaven rules and that God is still in control.

MEDITATION

When have you felt that circumstances in your life were out of control? How do you feel knowing that no matter how difficult your circumstances, and no matter what happens in this world, God is still in control?

GROW GRATEFUL
Give thanks that even when life seems out of control, God still reigns.

15 • *Grateful That God Is Holy*

Ascribe to Yahweh the glory due His name; worship
Yahweh in the splendor of His holiness.
PSALM 29:2

What's the most spectacular sight you've seen? I was recently in Niagara
Falls, which collectively refers to three magnificent waterfalls that
straddle the international border between Canada and the United
States. Standing at the base of the largest of the three, the Horseshoe
Falls, is a remarkable experience. One cannot help but be awestruck
by the beauty, power, and splendor of the thundering waters. I was
wowed.

Psalm 29:2 encourages us to ascribe glory—that is, worship, praise,
and thanksgiving—to God for the *splendor of His holiness*. The Bible
indicates there are three main facets to holiness. The first has to do
with moral excellence. To be holy is to be righteous and pure. Second,
holiness means to be "set apart." It means that something is uncommon
or extraordinary. Finally, the word *holy* means illustrious. To be holy is

to radiate and shine brightly. Holiness is inherently brilliant, dazzling, and magnificent. To be holy is to be spectacularly beautiful.

God's holiness is more spectacular, immaculate, compelling, and fearful than we can fathom. One theologian called God's holiness the *mysterium tremendum et fascinans*—the fearsome, fascinating mystery.[6] It's a mystery because it's a reality beyond our conception. It's fascinating because its beauty attracts and allures us, yet it's also fearsome because its dazzling purity causes us to tremble. Does the wonder and beauty of the Lord's holiness take your breath away? It should. Even the angels in heaven are overwhelmed with awe and ceaselessly exclaim, "Holy, holy, holy is the Lord God Almighty!" (Revelation 4:8).

MEDITATION

Why do you think Christians sometimes fail to be awestruck by the splendor of God's holiness? How can you cultivate a greater awareness of the holiness of God? How do you think a greater awareness might affect you?

GROW GRATEFUL
Praise God for the splendor of His holiness.

16 · *Grateful That God Is Wise*

> Wisdom and strength belong to God;
> counsel and understanding are His.
> JOB 12:13

How smart are you? Intelligence tests measure how smart a person is compared to the rest of the population. Average IQ (Intelligence Quotient) is about 100. Albert Einstein's IQ is estimated to have been about 160. People who have IQs higher than 140 are considered geniuses. Less than 1 percent of the world's population falls into the "genius" category.[7] Those who do can join Mensa, an elite organization whose membership is restricted to geniuses and near-geniuses.

But does a high IQ score mean that a person has the "smarts" for living? I once saw a comic that depicted a genius trying to get into the "Society for Geniuses" building. Though the door was clearly marked "push," the genius was pulling with all his might to open it. I think we would all agree that knowledge doesn't always translate into wisdom and understanding. Even geniuses struggle to make life work.

Thankfully, we don't need to despair at our lack of smarts or rely on our own limited know-how. We all have access to divine, omniscient, supernatural knowledge. God is rich in knowledge, understanding, and wisdom. His intellectual virtues are so great that even the thoughts and ideas of the brightest genius are foolish in comparison (1 Corinthians 1:25). "Now if any of you lacks wisdom," Scripture advises, "he should ask God, who gives to all generously and without criticizing, and it will be given to him" (James 1:5).

MEDITATION

How do you feel knowing that if you ask, God will give you wisdom "generously and without criticizing"? When have you asked and received wisdom from God? In what area of your life do you need wisdom, counsel, and understanding?

GROW GRATEFUL
Praise God for being rich in knowledge and generous to give you counsel.

17 · *Grateful That God Is Creative*

> You have made me rejoice, LORD, by what You
> have done; I will shout for joy because of the
> works of Your hands. How magnificent are Your
> works, LORD, how profound Your thoughts!
> PSALM 92:4–5

Many years ago, my husband, Brent, accompanied a friend to a local art show that had various paintings and pieces of art for sale. There, a small bronze sculpture captured Brent's fancy. The artist had used an ancient method of casting bronze that first appeared about 2000 BC and was prominent throughout the Bronze Age. Brent didn't know much about the sculptor who had created the work, but he was fascinated with the "lost-wax" method of casting he used, and with the detail, color, and artistry of his work. On a whim Brent bought the piece.

The French-Canadian artist, Joe Fafard, went on to have an illustrious career. The value of the sculpture Brent owned skyrocketed. And the way we thought about that piece of bronze changed too. It is far *more* than just a beautiful work of art—it is a sculpture created by the renowned Joe Fafard! Knowing the reputation, creativity, and skill of the artist made us appreciate the work on an even deeper level. Instead of just admiring the one piece of art, we experienced a growing admiration for the artist and his entire body of creative work.

Popular wisdom on cultivating gratitude encourages us to appreciate the spectacular beauty of a sunset, or the exquisite hue and delicacy of a blossom, or the majestic flight of an eagle. These are all breathtaking, to be sure. But our appreciation is so much deeper when we understand and acknowledge the reputation, creativity, skill, and fame of the Artist who is wowing us with the beautiful sight.

MEDITATION

When you see a beautiful scene displayed in nature, do you marvel at the skill and creativity of the Lord? Do you acknowledge that it is the work of His hands?

GROW GRATEFUL
Take some time today to be
wowed by God's artwork.

18 · *Grateful That God Is Happy*

You make known to me the path of life; in
your presence there is fullness of joy; at your
right hand are pleasures forevermore.

PSALM 16:11 ESV

Famed French philosopher and theologian Blaise Pascal claimed that
seeking happiness is integral to what it means to be human, and that
it is, in fact, the motive behind every action of every person who has
ever lived.

> All men seek happiness. This is without exception. Whatever dif-
> ferent means they employ, they all tend to this end. The cause of
> some going to war, and of others avoiding it, is the same desire in
> both, attended with different views. The will never takes the least
> step but to this object. This is the motive of every action of every
> man, even of those who hang themselves.[8]

Have you ever considered that your desire to be happy is a God-given yearning that was placed in your heart by an infinitely and supremely happy God? Many people think that God is like a somber, gloomy, and marginally grumpy old man who begrudges people having fun and enjoying life. But nothing could be further from the truth.

God is happy *beyond our wildest imagination*! He is the blessed (happy) Father (1 Timothy 1:11) who wants us to have a joy-filled, abundant life (John 10:10; 15:11) and eternally bask in His joy (Matthew 25:23). So the problem is not that we seek happiness but that we seek it in the wrong place. As today's verse attests, fullness of joy is found in God's presence. "Happy are the people whose God is Yahweh" (Psalm 144:15).

MEDITATION

How do you perceive God? Do you view Him as being happy beyond your wildest imagination? What have you been relying on as your source of happiness? What do you need to do in order to experience the joy and pleasure of His presence?

GROW GRATEFUL
Thank God for being so happy and joyful.

19 · *Grateful for God's Enormous Love*

Great is your love, higher than the heavens;
your faithfulness reaches to the skies.
Psalm 108:4 niv

One of the most popular novelty items in gift stores in the seventies was a cute, big-eyed, cream-colored resin figurine with its arms stretched out wide and engraved with the words "I love you this much!" It was a big seller around Valentine's Day. A man would gift one to his sweetheart to communicate the depth of his feelings. The stretched-out arms of the statue indicated that he loved her with his whole being—to the full extent of his capacity.

Children, especially, need to grasp how much they're loved. That's why dozens of bedtime books—like *I Love You Near and Far* by Marjorie Blain Parker or *I Love You to the Moon and Back* by Jamie Brooke—try to quantify a parent's love in a way that a child can understand. My favorite is the bestseller *I Love You More* by Laura Duksta. Colorful illustrations and rhymes talk about some of the big things in a child's world. The moms and dads reading the book affirm that their love for their child is even bigger.

The psalmist in today's verse uses the same sort of approach to quantify God's love. He indicates that God's love is bigger than the biggest thing we can think of. It is "higher than the heavens."

Just imagine. When God wants to express how much He loves you, He stretches out His arms past the billions of stars, comets, supernovas, and galaxies in His unfathomably large universe and says, "I love you this much." Indeed, He says, "I love you *even more*."

MEDITATION

How do you feel when you are reminded that God's love for you is higher than the heavens? Can you think of some other ways to quantify how much He loves you?

GROW GRATEFUL
Like the author of today's verse, affirm—in prayer—how much God loves you.

20 · Grateful for God's Extravagant Love

You, Lord, are a compassionate and gracious God,
slow to anger and rich in faithful love and truth.
PSALM 86:15

We learned yesterday that God's love is enormous—higher than the heavens! But there's something else about His love for which we can be grateful. His love supersedes a sentimental type of affection that's based solely on feelings. It's far more solid and reliable.

There's a rich, powerful word that's used hundreds of times throughout Old Testament Scripture to describe God's love: the Hebrew word *chesed*. Translators have used various English words to translate *chesed*: love, faithful love, steadfast love, unfailing love, great love, loyal love, mercy, faithfulness, kindness, and/or loving-kindness. Why so many different words? Because it's extraordinarily difficult to come up with an English equivalent for *chesed*. *Chesed* speaks of a love that is firmly rooted in God's character. This type of love involves a covenant commitment, loyalty, steadfastness, and strength as well as kindness, tenderness, and mercy. *Chesed* is the type of love that accepts moral obligation for the welfare of the person loved. It's a love that doesn't depend on the response or behavior of the receiver but rather on the steadfast character and commitment of the giver.

Chesed is an undeserved kind of love. It's a devoted kind of love. It's an extravagant kind of love. And, as we see in today's verse, God is *rich*—that is, abounding—in it. Aren't you thankful that God loves you with this amazing kind of love? You don't need to question or doubt how He feels. His love for you is steadfast and true.

MEDITATION

Have you fully embraced the fact that God's love for you is enormous, extravagant, and loyal? Which aspect of His *chesed* love amazes you the most?

GROW GRATEFUL
Tell God what you appreciate about His love.

21 · *Grateful That God Is Faithful*

Because of the LORD's faithful love we do not perish, for His mercies never end. They are new every morning; great is Your faithfulness!
LAMENTATIONS 3:22–23

Thomas Chisholm was born in a log cabin in Kentucky in 1866. He was educated in a simple country schoolhouse, and at age sixteen he began to teach there. Wanting to have a greater impact, he served as a Methodist minister for one year at age thirty-six. But ill health made it impossible for him to continue. For the rest of his life he worked a desk job as a life insurance agent. By all accounts, his life was ordinary and unremarkable. But Thomas loved to write poetry. Over the years he filled his journals with hundreds of poems. When he was almost sixty, he decided to send a few to a friend who worked at a Christian music publisher. His friend was so moved by the words of Thomas's poem "Great Is Thy Faithfulness" that he put the words to music. Soon Thomas's poem about the faithfulness of God came to be known and loved in churches all around the world.

God's love and care for you never end. Because of this, you can have, in the words of the hymn, "strength for today and bright hope for tomorrow." Your day may be ordinary and humdrum. Or it may be filled with all sorts of challenges. It may be busy or boring, happy or sad. You don't always know what the day will bring. But you can be certain that it will be filled with plenty of God's mercy. His mercies to you are new every morning. Great is His faithfulness!

MEDITATION

What mercies do you see in your life today? How do you feel about the fact that God's mercies never end and are new every morning? In what way has He been faithful to you?

GROW GRATEFUL
Thank God for His faithfulness to you.

22 · *Grateful That God Is Just*

> LORD, You have heard the desire of the humble; You
> will strengthen their hearts. You will listen carefully,
> doing justice for the fatherless and the oppressed.
> PSALM 10:17–18

The newly installed sign read: No PARKING. MON TO FRI. 8:00–17:00.
SEPT TO JUNE. EXCEPT RESIDENTS. I read all the fine print. I was
a resident, though I was driving a borrowed vehicle. What's more,
though it was the first day of school for the students down the street,
the calendar informed me that I wouldn't need to flip to September
until the following day. Clearly I could park there.

Imagine my consternation when I discovered that an overly exuberant bylaw officer disagreed. He left a pale-yellow parking ticket
fluttering on the windshield. *What? That's not fair!* I was a resident.
And it was August, not September. Several phone calls and much
aggravation later, I finally managed to have the fine repealed.

Have you ever encountered a situation that was blatantly unfair?

It's natural to feel indignation when we see a miscarriage of justice. It's wrong for innocent parties to be punished for doing right and for perpetrators to get away with doing wrong. We all know that justice should be properly served. Aren't you grateful that righteousness and justice are the foundation of God's throne? God hears you when you cry out for justice. He listens carefully to your plea. And though His answer may not come how and when you expect, you can be confident that He will be fair and execute justice with perfect judgment. Human laws and courts sometimes fail, but "the LORD loves justice and will not abandon His faithful ones" (Psalm 37:28).

MEDITATION

Have you ever been denied justice? When have you felt indignation over an apparent miscarriage of justice? How do you feel knowing that the Lord loves justice and will not abandon His faithful ones?

GROW GRATEFUL
Thank God that He rules with justice.

23 · *Grateful That God Is Patient*

> The LORD is gracious and compassionate,
> slow to anger and great in faithful love.
> PSALM 145:8

Have you ever witnessed road rage? Once, a burly man in a truck started angrily gesturing and screaming at me. I'm not even sure what I did to rouse his fury. Perhaps I cut him off. Or perhaps I did something else wrong. But his behavior left no doubt in my mind as to how he felt. Then, as if obscene gestures and expletives weren't enough, he began to aggressively tailgate me. It wasn't until I turned into the parking lot of a nearby police station that he stopped his enraged pursuit.

I'm glad that God is not like that angry, impatient man. Scripture repeatedly affirms that He is *slow to anger* (Exodus 34:6; Nehemiah 9:17). When it comes to being provoked, He's extremely tolerant and puts up with a lot. That's not to say that wrongdoers will forever go unpunished (Nahum 1:3). Rather, He gives people ample opportunity to avoid this fate. Peter explained, "The Lord does not delay His promise, as some understand delay, but is patient with you, not wanting any to perish but all to come to repentance" (2 Peter 3:9).

The patience of God ought to give you great comfort and confidence. If you do something wrong, He won't respond like that hothead in the truck. He will be patient with you. You can run toward Him rather than away from Him. You can draw near without fear, knowing that He will not respond in anger but with mercy and grace (Hebrews 4:16).

MEDITATION

Do you think of God as being angry and impatient or as patient and even tempered? Where do you think you got this concept of God? How do you feel knowing that God is patient with wrongdoers? How do you feel knowing that God is patient with you?

GROW GRATEFUL
Thank God that He is patient and slow to anger.

24 · *Grateful That God Is Kind*

> So that in the coming ages He might display
> the immeasurable riches of His grace through
> His kindness to us in Christ Jesus.
> EPHESIANS 2:7

"Practice random acts of kindness and senseless acts of beauty" is a famous quote from the early 1980s. No one is exactly sure who first said it. Regardless, the idea caught on like wildfire. It wasn't long before the saying was plastered on bumper stickers and T-shirts everywhere. The Random Acts of Kindness Foundation was established in 1995 to encourage the practice of kindness. Even Congress joined in, declaring an entire week in February as National Random Acts of Kindness Week. When that week rolls around each year, we're reminded to do kind things, like hold the door open for someone, pay bridge tolls for cars behind us, wave to kids in school buses, or pay someone an unexpected compliment. The "random acts of kindness" movement is a powerful commentary on the state of our society. A kind person is

truly a rare find. Our lives are so filled with selfish pursuits that we crave those moments when someone breaks the norm and is benevolent toward us.

To be kind is to have a good heart that is inclined toward doing kind things for others. The Bible teaches that kindness originates with God and is defined by who He is and what He does. God is infinitely kind. Christ's appearance on earth was the most profound expression of His kindness (Titus 3:4). In a world where we see far more takers than givers, the kindness of God draws us like a magnet. It's the beautiful trait that attracts us to Him (Romans 2:4).

MEDITATION

Who is the kindest person you know? When was a time you were deeply affected by someone's kindness toward you? How did you feel? How did you respond? Does God's kindness affect you the same way?

GROW GRATEFUL
Thank God for His great kindness.

25 · *Grateful That God Is Merciful*

The LORD is good to all, and his mercy
is over all that he has made.
PSALM 145:9 ESV

The small vehicle parked on the street was buried in a thick, fresh layer
of snow. That's why I failed to notice it when I backed up my truck.
The sudden thud and crunch alerted me to the fact that something
was wrong. My heart sank when I jumped out and saw that I had
broken the side mirror off a car. Since the car was parked in front of
an apartment building, there was no way of knowing who the owner
was. So I scrawled my name and phone number on a scrap of paper
and left the note under the windshield wiper. The owner was glad
that I confessed. The estimate was far higher than I expected—almost
a thousand dollars—but I agreed to pay for the repairs. The next
day the man called back with some surprising news. He had found a

replacement part at a junkyard and would fix the car himself. I didn't have to pay. My debt was forgiven.

The encounter reminds me of how God covers our debt (Colossians 2:14). Because of His rich mercy, we don't have to "pay up." He paid for the damage caused by our sins. The debt I owed the owner of that car was relatively small. But just imagine how overwhelmed and grateful I felt when he forgave it. When you ponder God's goodness toward you, and how He mercifully forgives the great debt of sin, I am certain that you will feel even more overwhelmed and grateful.

MEDITATION

When has someone demonstrated mercy toward you? How did you feel about receiving their undeserved favor? Is your gratitude to God proportionate to the mercy you've received from Him? Why or why not?

GROW GRATEFUL
Thank God for being so merciful.

26 · *Grateful for the New Covenant*

> In the same way He also took the cup after supper and said, "This cup is the new covenant established by My blood; it is shed for you."
> LUKE 22:20

Your Bible is made up of two sections—the Old and the New Testament. A testament is a covenant. The New Testament speaks about the *new* covenant God established through Jesus. You may wonder, *What exactly is a covenant?* and *What makes the new covenant different than the old?*

A covenant is a contract. It's a legal term that describes a formal and binding declaration of benefits to be given by one party to another and the conditions attached. The old covenant was God's agreement with the ancient Israelites. He promised to bless and protect them if they obeyed His righteous laws. There were hundreds and hundreds of laws. No one could possibly keep them all. But God made allowance for their failures by instituting a system of repeated, daily animal sacrifices to atone for their sins.

This system of animal sacrifice was only temporary. It foreshadowed the time when Jesus Christ would sacrifice Himself and resolve the problem of sin once and for all. His death and resurrection ushered in a new agreement between God and all people. In the new covenant, Jesus satisfies *all* the conditions. Our only obligation is to put our faith in Him. What's more, now, instead of being obliged to follow a list of external rules, God writes those rules directly on our hearts through the indwelling presence of His Holy Spirit. He meets all the conditions of the covenant for us, and then He showers us with divine benefits and blessings. Thank You, God, for the new covenant!

MEDITATION

How is the new agreement better than the old? What are some benefits and blessings you've received from God? How do you think your life would change if you more fully grasped what Jesus has done for you?

GROW GRATEFUL
Thank God for His new covenant through Jesus.

27 · *Grateful That God Saves Me*

Everyone who calls on the name
of the Lord will be saved.

ROMANS 10:13

Two Florida teenagers were swimming at a local beach in Jacksonville when a strong current swept them out miles from shore. They tried to swim back toward land, but the rough seas and currents hampered their efforts. Without life vests, they struggled to stay afloat. Exhausted, frightened, and certain they'd soon be overcome by waves, they grabbed each other's hands and began to call out to God for help. That's when Eric Wagner's boat, named *Amen*, appeared. It reached the teens just in time. Neither had enough strength left to climb in. Had the *Amen* not come, they surely would have drowned.[9]

The story illustrates our spiritual predicament. None of us has what it takes to overcome the powerful waves of sin. We are all dead in our trespasses and in need of a Savior. The good news is that when we cry out to God, He comes to our aid. The *Amen* rescues us. "Everyone who calls on the name of the Lord will be saved."

After their drowning scare, the teens profusely thanked Wagner for rescuing them. In interviews, they lauded his swift action and compassion. I expect that they'll speak of the rescue and sing his praise for the rest of their lives. Gratitude and praise are the natural response to being saved. Which begs the question: Is your heart filled with gratitude and praise for the One who has saved your soul?

MEDITATION

When did you call out to the Lord to be saved? Since you were rescued, what changes have you seen in your life? After you are saved, why do you need to continue to rely on God for help?

GROW GRATEFUL
Thank God for saving you.

28 · *Grateful That God Redeems Me*

We have redemption in Him through His
blood, the forgiveness of our trespasses,
according to the riches of His grace.
EPHESIANS 1:7

When my mother was young, her family owned a mischievous, lovable
mutt of a dog named Mollie. Mollie's adventures are legendary. He
was always getting into trouble. His escapades have been told and
retold around my mother's dinner table. Mollie disliked boots. Anyone
walking past the house with boots would end up with toothmarks in
the leather. Mollie stole links of sausage from the village butcher. He
destroyed neighbors' gardens. Naturally, Grandpa paid for the damage. The village dogcatchers were always running after Mollie with
nets. Usually he managed to evade them. But twice Grandpa also had
to pay the fee to redeem Mollie from the dogcatcher's wagon.

My grandpa was Mollie's redeemer. He repeatedly paid the price to set his scoundrel of a dog free. To *redeem* means to buy back, to remove an obligation by payment, or to release from blame or debt. It's the liberation of any possession, object, or person by payment of a ransom. In Greek, the root word means "to loose or set free."[10]

Redemption is one of the most profound and central truths of Scripture. God redeems us. He pays the debt we owe for sin. Like Grandpa paying the ransom to get Mollie out of the back of the dog-catcher's cage, Christ's sacrifice buys us back and sets us free. And just like Mollie's exuberant response when the door of the cage opened, our hearts ought to be full of joy and gratitude that Jesus has redeemed us and set us free.

MEDITATION

Think about the price Christ paid to secure your freedom. According to Ephesians 1:7, why did He do this? How do you feel about what Christ did for you? How does His sacrifice affect your behavior?

GROW GRATEFUL
Thank God for setting you free.

29 · *Grateful That God Forgives Me*

> Joyful is the one whose transgression is
> forgiven, whose sin is covered!
> PSALM 32:1

Simon was mortified. A woman of ill repute had crashed his party and was making a terrible scene. Wanting to impress, Simon had invited Jesus over for dinner. But this ignoble woman kneeled at His feet wetting them with her tears. Even worse, then she wiped them with her hair, kissed them, and anointed them with costly, fragrant oil (Luke 7:37–38). The woman was a prostitute, and the perfume may well have been part of her trade. Simon scorned her fanatical display of gratitude and affection. He was even more perturbed that Jesus didn't put an end to it.

Jesus could tell what Simon was thinking. He responded, "He who is forgiven little, loves little" (v. 47). His point was not that some people sin less than others and need less forgiveness. Rather, that a person's gratitude is proportionate to their awareness of how much God has done for them. Simon's problem was that he had no concept of how sinful his heart really was. He didn't consider his sins to be terribly serious or many. He didn't think that he needed much forgiveness. The woman, on the other hand, was keenly aware of how much she needed forgiveness—and how much she needed Jesus.

Our gratitude is affected by our awareness of the depth of our need. It's also affected by our awareness of the extent of Christ's forgiveness. We have all been forgiven much. And we have all been forgiven completely. Therefore, we should all respond to God's forgiveness with much gratitude and love.

MEDITATION

Do you think the woman's sin was worse than Simon's? Why do you think Simon failed to realize that he needed forgiveness just as much as she did? Is your attitude more like his or more like hers?

GROW GRATEFUL
Thank God for forgiving your sin.

30 · Grateful That God Cleanses Me

> How joyful is the one whose transgression is forgiven. . . .
> Wash away my guilt and cleanse me from my sin.
>
> PSALM 32:1; 51:2

One summer my niece invited me and all the other adult women in our family to join her in a six-kilometer Mud Hero obstacle run for charity. The name of the race says it all. Mud. Oodles of mud. Mud everywhere. We slid down muddy slopes into mud pits. Waded through muddy lagoons. Crawled on our bellies in mud under cargo nets. Wound our way through a mud forest. Conquered more mud obstacles. And finally made it to the final pit to soak in our victory mud bath.

The race was fun, but by the end all I wanted to do was to get clean. Never in my life have I been so dirty. I was caked in mud. It had invaded every possible crevice of my body. The wash-off hoses helped. Some. But my clothing and running shoes were unredeemable.

Though I washed and washed, there was simply no way to get all the dirt out. I ended up throwing them away.

Sin does to our hearts what that mud did to my clothing. We feel dirty. Unclean. Damaged. And no matter how we try, we can't get rid of the grime. But thankfully, Jesus does not toss us aside. He takes away the stain of sin, guilt, and shame and makes us squeaky clean. "'Come, let us discuss this,' says the LORD. 'Though your sins are like scarlet, they will be as white as snow; though they are as red as crimson, they will be like wool'" (Isaiah 1:18).

MEDITATION

When have you felt guilt and shame? How did you deal with those feelings? How do you feel knowing that God forgives your sin, washes away your guilt, and makes you clean? What sin do you need to be cleansed of today?

GROW GRATEFUL
Praise God for washing away your sin and making you clean.

31 · *Grateful That God Accepts Me*

No condemnation now exists for those in Christ Jesus.
ROMANS 8:1

How many thoughts go through your mind each day? Maybe one thousand? Five thousand? Ten thousand? According to the Laboratory of Neuro Imaging at the University of Southern California, the average person thinks about 48.6 thoughts per minute. That adds up to a staggering total of seventy thousand thoughts per day. Some of these thoughts are conscious and intentional, but many come uninvited and pass through our minds at lightning speed.[11]

Researchers also say that, of all the thoughts that pass through the average person's mind each day, about 95 percent are the same repetitive thoughts the person had the day before, and about 80 percent are negative in nature.[12] That's a lot of negative mental chatter! Deep down, people are much more self-condemning, insecure, pessimistic, and fearful than their sunny social media updates lead us to believe.

Many of us suffer from feelings of inadequacy and inferiority.

What's more, we suspect that God views us the same way we view ourselves. We think, *How could He possibly accept someone like me?* But Scripture tells us there is *no condemnation* for those in Christ Jesus. None. That doesn't mean that God approves of sinful behavior, but it does mean that He has completely accounted for the problem of your sin. Once you have repented from your sin, He does not hold it against you. He does not condemn you. He does not disapprove of you. He loves and accepts you completely, just the way you are. You can approach the throne of grace with boldness, knowing that you are fully accepted by God (Hebrews 4:16).[13]

MEDITATION

Do you struggle with feelings of inadequacy and inferiority? How often each day do you suspect that you are not good enough or that people don't accept you? Why can you be confident that you are fully loved and accepted by God?

GROW GRATEFUL
Thank God that He loves and accepts you completely.

32 · Grateful That God Adopts Me

He destined us for adoption as his children through
Jesus Christ, according to the good pleasure of his will.
EPHESIANS 1:5 NRSV

Michael Oher was a disadvantaged teen who became an All-American
football player and first-round NFL draft pick. Michael was put into
the foster care system at age seven, where he was bounced around from
house to house. His life was headed in a dangerous direction when he
met the Tuohy family. They befriended him, fed him, clothed him,
helped him with his studies, gave him a home, and adopted him as their
own. The Tuohys gave Michael what he never had before—a loving,
stable family, a sense of belonging, and an opportunity to thrive. With
his adoptive parents and siblings cheering him on, he was able to achieve
his dreams of an NFL career and a Super Bowl ring.

Michael's story is a great illustration for what happens when God
adopts us. Adoption, in New Testament times, was a legal change
in status that gave a son the right to the name and the citizenship of

the father, and the right to inherit his property. When you believe in Jesus, you become part of God's family and get all sorts of benefits and blessings. You get a Dad who loves you and cheers you on. A family where you can experience a sense of belonging. Bountiful resources at your disposal. As part of God's family, you get everything you need in order to thrive! Aren't you grateful that you've been adopted by God?

MEDITATION

What does it mean to have the legal right to our heavenly Father's name, citizenship, and property? What are some family benefits and blessings that God showers on His children? How can these benefits help you thrive?

GROW GRATEFUL
Thank God for adopting
you into His family.

33 · Grateful That God Fathers Me

> Because you are sons, God has sent the Spirit of
> His Son into our hearts, crying, "Abba, Father!"
> GALATIANS 4:6

Juan lived in a small town in Spain. He was wild and rebellious. In his teen years, he stole a large sum of money from his father and ran away from home. Nevertheless, the father loved his son and longed for him to return. Months passed. When the father got word that someone had seen Juan in the city, he went there to search for him. He drove up and down the streets, showed Juan's picture to strangers, and checked in bars, but to no avail.

Finally, an idea struck him. He took out an ad in the local paper. It said, "Juan, all is forgiven. How I long to see you again. Please meet me on Saturday at noon on the steps of city hall. Love, Dad."

When Saturday came and the father went to the appointed place, he found, along with his son, more than a hundred other boys named Juan sitting on the steps of city hall. All the boys were longing, yearning, to have a relationship with the fathers from whom they were estranged.[14]

The human need to be fathered is deep. The longing expressed by those boys is reminiscent of the longing that resides in each of our hearts. Our spirits long to be fathered by the father of our dreams, our perfect heavenly Father. And when He adopts us into His family, that dream becomes a reality. We come to know Him as our loving Abba, Father—our Daddy.

MEDITATION

What do you think it means when the psalmist says God is a Father to the fatherless (Psalm 68:5)? Do you relate to God as Father? Why or why not? Think of the ways God fathers you. For which aspect of His fathering are you the most grateful?

GROW GRATEFUL
Thank God for the ways in which He fathers you.

34 · *Grateful That God Is My Friend*

> LORD, You have searched me and known me. . . .
> You are aware of all my ways. . . . You have encircled
> me; You have placed Your hand on me. This
> extraordinary knowledge is beyond me. It is lofty.
> PSALM 139:1–6

Loneliness poses a major health risk. It can disrupt sleep, raise blood pressure, lower immunity, increase depression, and significantly shorten a person's lifespan. Experts warn that loneliness has become a worldwide epidemic.[15] The feeling of being unwanted, uncared for, and alone is a problem more widespread than diabetes or cancer.

Having many friends doesn't guarantee that you'll have a good or close friend. You can be surrounded by a crowd and still feel lonely. Solomon wrote a proverb about that: "A man with many friends may be harmed, but there is a friend who stays closer than a brother" (Proverbs

18:24). Maybe Solomon picked up this saying from his father, David, who experienced both situations. David had many friends abandon and betray him. But his friend Jonathan, whose soul "was knit to the soul of David," remained true to the end (1 Samuel 18:1 ESV).

Many theologians suggest the proverb also alludes to the type of friend we have in God. *He* is the friend who stays closer than a brother. According to today's passage, He knows you completely. He knows everything about you. He understands your thoughts. He's aware of all your ways. He encircles you and has placed His hand on you. He will never ignore you, abandon you, betray you, or disappoint you. Whenever you feel lonely, remember that you have a Friend who stays closer than a brother. In Jesus, you have the best Friend a person could ever hope for!

MEDITATION

How did the psalmist feel about the fact that God knew and understood him and was aware of all his ways? Do you feel that God knows and understands you in the same way? Do you regard God as your Friend? How might His friendship be a remedy for your loneliness?

GROW GRATEFUL
Pray Psalm 139:1–6 as a personal prayer of gratitude to God.

35 · Grateful That God Delights in Me

> Yahweh your God is among you, a warrior who saves. He will rejoice over you with gladness. He will bring you quietness with His love. He will delight in you with shouts of joy.
>
> Zephaniah 3:17

One of the things I love most about my young grandchildren is their joyful exuberance. Whenever I go to their house, I am met with squeals and shouts of delight. They run and jump for joy, slather me with hugs and kisses, and repeatedly exclaim, "*Omi! Omi!*" (the German word for Granny). Their delight at my arrival leaves no doubt in my mind about how they feel about me. It warms my heart and makes me smile.

Earlier we meditated on the truth that God is a happy God. This happiness spills over into how He responds to us. As today's verse indicates, He rejoices over us with gladness. He delights in us with shouts of joy. Another Bible version reads, "He will exult over you with loud singing" (ESV). *Loud* singing! Have you ever pictured God as exuberantly bursting into loud singing? And have you ever considered that He does this over you?

Zephaniah 3:17 isn't the only verse in Scripture that indicates that God delights in us. Psalm 149:4 tells us that the Lord "takes pleasure" in His people. "Faithful people are His delight" (Proverbs 12:22). He calls His faithful ones "*Hepzibah*," an affectionate name that means "My delight in you" (Isaiah 62:4). Even creation joins in God's joyful exuberance. "The mountains and the hills will break into singing before you, and all the trees of the field will clap their hands" (55:12). Are you amazed when you consider that you bring such joy to God's heart?

MEDITATION

Take a moment to imagine God rejoicing over you with gladness and delighting in you with loud singing and shouts of joy. How does this make you feel? If you truly believed God delighted in you, how would that affect your life?

GROW GRATEFUL
Thank God that He delights in you with
shouts of joy and loud singing.

36 · Grateful That God Cheers Me

> You give him blessings forever; You cheer
> him with joy in Your presence.
> PSALM 21:6

In Steven Spielberg's 1991 movie *Hook*, the unimaginable has happened. Peter Pan, the boy who would not grow up, has grown up to be a cutthroat merger and acquisitions lawyer. Wrapped up in his career, Peter neglects his wife and two children and has forgotten all about his childhood exploits. Peter's old nemesis, Captain Hook, kidnaps Peter's children to force him to come back to Neverland for one final battle. To avoid certain defeat, Tinkerbell and the Lost Boys must jog Peter's memory and help him regain Neverland's magic. The defining moment comes when Peter searches for a "happy thought" to help him fly. It dawns on him that his greatest joy is being a father. His children, Jack and Maggie, are his happy thought. This realization changes everything. It enables Peter to fly, defeat Hook, rescue his children, and save the day. The lesson for Peter is that people, rather than possessions or pursuits, are our greatest source of joy.

One of my happy thoughts is my grandchildren. Thinking of them always brings a smile to my face. You likely have people in your life who do the same for you. According to Psalm 21:6, being with God has an even more profound effect. He gives us blessings—happy things—forever. He cheers us with inexpressible joy in His presence. Earlier we learned that God delights in us. The feeling can be mutual. God can become your "happy thought"—the One who cheers you with joy as you delight in *Him*.

MEDITATION

How can our possessions and pursuits cause us to neglect important relationships? Have you forgotten that God is your happy thought? How can you be cheered with joy in His presence today?

GROW GRATEFUL
Thank God that He
cheers you with joy.

37 · *Grateful for God's Abundant Grace*

Indeed, we have all received grace
after grace from His fullness.
JOHN 1:16

My granddaughter was elated when a gentleman gave her a bike. We were walking past his house, and he was clearing away unsold garage sale items. "Do you have a bike?" he called out. Upon learning she didn't, he held out a pink princess bike. "Here, take it!" I offered to pay, but he refused. He was happy to give it away. Though he was probably just ridding his garage of unwanted items, we were delighted by this unexpected gift.

God offers His gifts free of charge. We do not need to earn them or pay for them. He gives us grace after grace. *Grace* is the English translation of a Greek word (*charis*), from which we also get the word *charity*. *Charis* is a favor that brings delight, joy, happiness, or good fortune.[16] It's a free, no-strings-attached gift, which is motivated only by the generosity and big-heartedness of the giver.

The Lord lavishes *riches* of grace on you (Ephesians 1:7–8). He is neither stingy nor cheap. That's why at the wedding Jesus provided an overabundance of wine, at the picnic an overabundance of bread, and in the net an overabundance of fish (John 2:7; Mark 6:43; Luke 5:6). He will make "*all* grace abound to you . . . in *all* things, at *all* times" (2 Corinthians 9:8 ESV, emphasis added). You will receive one gift after another from your extravagant, big-hearted heavenly Father.

MEDITATION

Is there a relationship or situation in your life for which you currently need God's grace? How do you think His promise of *all* grace in *all* things at *all* times might help you?

GROW GRATEFUL
Thank God for His lavish, extravagant grace.

38 · Grateful for God's Wonderful Deeds

> Give thanks to Yahweh, call on His name;
> proclaim His deeds among the peoples.
> PSALM 105:1

The Jews called the book of Psalms "the Hallel," which means "the book of praises." Psalm 136 is a special psalm known as the *Great* Hallel. The people of Israel sang this great psalm of praise together liturgically when they celebrated Passover, a major annual festival in the temple at Jerusalem. The leader of the choir would cite a reason to thank God, and the people would respond with the refrain, "For His steadfast love endures forever!" (ESV).

> Give thanks to the LORD, for he is good . . . For his
> steadfast love endures forever.
> Give thanks to the God of gods . . . For his steadfast love
> endures forever.

Give thanks to the Lord of lords . . . For his steadfast love endures forever. (vv. 1–3)

There are twenty-three more couplets in this psalm. The Israelites praised God for His creation. They praised Him for remembering them and taking pity on them. They praised Him for how He delivered them from bondage. They praised Him for His help in battle, for giving them victory over opponents, and for leading them to the promised land. They praised Him for His ongoing care and provision.

The psalm essentially recounts the history of their journey with God, recalling how He had blessed them along the way. How has He blessed you? Think of times when He demonstrated His faithfulness. As you recall His wonderful works in your life, thank Him that His steadfast love for you endures forever.

MEDITATION

What are the major events in your journey with God for which you are thankful? How often do you look back to remember and give thanks? Set aside some time to compose your own Great Hallel.

* * * * * * *

GROW GRATEFUL
Thank God for His wonderful works on your behalf.

39 · Grateful That God Created Me

It was You who created my inward parts; You knit me together in my mother's womb. I will praise You because I have been remarkably and wonderfully made. Your works are wonderful, and I know this very well.

PSALM 139:13–14

The colorful and unique assortment of handmade vases, pitchers, cups, and bowls displayed in the window of the pottery shop was lovely. A small sign taped in the corner offered a complimentary lesson on how to use a pottery wheel. How hard could it be? I was certain I could create a masterpiece equally beautiful. So I confidently signed up.

First, I wedged the clay to get all the air pockets out and ensure that the lump was uniform in stiffness. Next, I smacked the clay down as close to the middle of the wheel as possible. Then, with wet, clay-coated hands I tried to shape the spinning lump into a pot. Though I tried my best, my container ended up looking crude and lopsided—nothing like the works of art produced by the store owner. By the time I finished my lesson, it was clear to me that her skill far surpassed mine.

The Bible depicts God as the Master Potter. He lovingly forms each one of us like a potter shapes clay. "LORD, You are our Father; we are the clay, and You are our potter; we all are the work of Your hands" (Isaiah 64:8). Unlike my amateur attempts at forming a pot, God doesn't make mistakes. He expertly crafted your inward parts. Like a skilled artisan, He knit you together in your mother's womb. You have been remarkably and wonderfully made. Your uniqueness testifies to His hands-on involvement in your creation and His ongoing interest in your life.

MEDITATION

How do you feel when you consider that you are the work of God's hands? Do you agree that you have been remarkably and wonderfully made? Are you grateful that His design for you is intentional and not accidental?

GROW GRATEFUL
Thank God that you are the work of His hands.

40 · Grateful That God Sees Me

> She called the name of the LORD who spoke to
> her, "You are a God of seeing," for she said, "Truly
> here I have seen him who looks after me."
>
> GENESIS 16:13 ESV

Hagar was an Egyptian handmaid who was forced to become a surrogate for her Hebrew mistress, Sarah. When the pregnancy was confirmed, Sarah began to treat the teen with open contempt. Pregnant, and feeling helpless and alone, Hagar decided to run away from Sarah's constant abuse. On her way back to Egypt, Hagar stopped to rest at a spring in the desert. The angel of the Lord met her there. He assured her of God's protection and blessing. Hagar was astonished. She thought no one saw or understood her desperate predicament. But God did. Overwhelmed by this new awareness, Hagar exclaimed, "You are El Roi!" which means "the God who sees."

God saw Hagar and God sees you. You are not alone. Your troubles never go unnoticed. He sees the tears you silently cry in the dark. He collects each one in His bottle (Psalm 56:8). He sees your frustrations, your disappointments, and your troubles. He sees your heartaches and your longings. And not only does He see and know everything about you, He also cares about you. When Hagar met God at the spring, she discovered that God had been looking after her all along. "Truly here I have seen him who looks after me." Regardless of the challenges you face, know that you are seen by God. He sees you. He cares for you. He looks after you. "The eyes of the Lord are on the righteous, and His ears are open to their cry for help" (Psalm 34:15).

MEDITATION

How might knowing you are seen by God affect your attitude and behavior? When have you felt alone and unseen? How do you feel knowing that God sees all your troubles?

GROW GRATEFUL
Thank God that His eyes are on you and that His ears are open to your cry.

41 · Grateful That God Cares for Me

Praise be to the God and Father of our Lord
Jesus Christ, the Father of compassion.

2 CORINTHIANS 1:3 NIV

My father was a prisoner of war in World War II. Though it was winter, he was stripped of his jacket and boots and marched in bare feet across Europe for weeks. When his physical condition deteriorated to the point where he could no longer walk, he was thrown in a barn with other wounded soldiers. Dad was gravely ill and malnourished. He had severe frostbite, and gangrene was setting in. But through his delirium, he saw a Russian guard approach and kneel by his side. She cradled his swollen feet and gently lanced the tough black ulcers. Were it not for this unusual kindness, he would have certainly been overcome by infection and died. He has never forgotten that act of compassion.

God is *the Father of compassion*. Compassion is a feeling of deep sympathy and sorrow for someone who has been stricken by misfortune, accompanied by a strong desire to alleviate the suffering. God not only sees the human plight; He is also keen to intervene. Compassion is what moved Jesus to heal diseases and infirmities, cast out demons, raise the dead, forgive sins, and make the broken whole. "When He saw the crowds, He felt compassion for them" (Matthew 9:36). Don't think for a moment that God feels cold and indifferent toward you. When He sees your hurts and struggles, His heart is stirred with empathy. He yearns to help. Because of His deep compassion, you can boldly approach Him in your time of need.

MEDITATION

When have you wondered whether God was indifferent toward the challenges and difficulties in your life? How do you feel, knowing that He cares and is moved with compassion for you?

GROW GRATEFUL
Thank the Lord that He has
compassion on you.

42 · *Grateful That God Comforts Me*

> [Praise] the God of all comfort. He comforts us in all our affliction. . . . For as the sufferings of Christ overflow to us, so through Christ our comfort also overflows.
>
> 2 CORINTHIANS 1:3–5

The apostle Paul had to deal with far more trouble than most. He was imprisoned, beaten, stoned, and shipwrecked. His enemies wanted to kill him. He faced dangers everywhere he went. He was overworked and experienced significant hardships and many sleepless nights. He often lived without adequate finances, food, and clothing. Not only that, he keenly felt the ongoing burden and responsibility of caring for all the churches (2 Corinthians 11:23–28).

Paul knew what it meant to suffer. But when he felt the weight and burden of his troubles, God comforted him. Paul was undoubtedly speaking from experience when he praised *the God of all comfort who comforts us in all our affliction*. The English word *comfort* can indicate emotional relief and the reduction of pain and suffering. But the Greek word is more closely connected with the Latin root *fortis*, which means brave, strong, and courageous. The type of comfort Paul received from God gave him courage. It didn't spare him from difficulty, but it enabled him to be brave and strong to face every trial.

Your story may be different from the apostle Paul's. But I'm sure you also face difficulties from time to time. Isn't it good to know that whenever you feel the weight and burden of your troubles, you can find comfort in God? He cares about your pain and suffering. When you turn to Him with your heartaches, His comfort will give you courage and make you brave and strong.

MEDITATION

When have you received comfort from God? Why is God's comfort crucial during times of difficulty? For which circumstance or difficulty do you currently need God's comfort?

GROW GRATEFUL
Thank God for comforting you in times of difficulty.

43 · Grateful That God Walks with Me

"Do not fear, for I have redeemed you; I have
called you by your name; you are Mine. I will be
with you when you pass through the waters."
Isaiah 43:1–2

Twelve young boys and their coach set out after football practice one day
to spend a few hours exploring the caves of Tham Luang, Thailand.
Most of the year, the seven-mile twisting channel of limestone tunnels,
nooks, and crannies is relatively dry. But during rainy season, the narrow passageways can fill with water, making the caves impossible to
navigate. The boys wanted to squeeze in one last adventure before the
monsoons came. But during their exploit, a heavy rain hit, trapping
them deep inside.

What was supposed to be a short excursion turned into a massive
two-week-long search-and-rescue operation and the most extraordinary

cave rescue in history. For the rescue, each boy was tethered to a lead diver, who shared oxygen with him and dragged him along—wading, climbing, and diving through the cold, murky water and airless chambers. All the boy needed to do was to lay still and trust the diver to get him through the treacherous passage.

A journey with God is like that. He will remain tethered to you when you pass through the difficult passages of life. You don't need to be afraid of dark and difficult tunnels. He has called you by your name; you are His. You can count on His presence and His protection. Like the diver pulling the boy through the long, twisting channel, you can count on Him to guide you through all the turns of life. He will walk with you and see you safely through.

MEDITATION

How can you tether yourself to God? Why is it important to trust Him when you pass through difficult waters? How can you combat the anxiety that facing such situations can cause?

GROW GRATEFUL

Thank God for always walking with you.

44 · Grateful That God Protects Me

You have been my help, and in the shadow
of your wings I will sing for joy.
PSALM 63:7 ESV

The wood stork is a large, heavy-billed bird that wades in the shallow
waters of Southern swamps. Storks are known for being dedicated parents. If you happen upon a wood stork rookery—a place where groups
of these birds make nests and raise their young—you might observe a
mother bird spreading out her wing to shade her babies from the hot
sun. Or she might shelter them under her wings to protect them from
rain, or from danger, or to keep them warm.

It's common for baby birds to take shelter in their mama's
shadow—either under her wings or directly under her, in her brood
patch. The brood patch is a warm, soft, fluid-filled area on a mother's
belly. Babies can snuggle in this space and be surrounded by the cushy

comfort of their mother's body. There is no safer or more comfortable place for a baby bird to be.

Scripture often uses the metaphor of God as a mighty bird, encouraging us to run to Him for protection like a baby bird takes shelter under its mother. "He will cover you with His feathers; you will take refuge under His wings. His faithfulness will be a protective shield" (Psalm 91:3–4). David, the author of these verses, made a habit of dwelling in God's shadow. And you can too. There's plenty of room. Whenever you need comfort or protection you can run to Him and be kept safe and warm in the shelter of His wings.

MEDITATION

What do you like about the imagery of hiding under the shadow of God's wings? How often do you metaphorically do this? Why is it important that you learn to run to Him for shelter and protection?

GROW GRATEFUL
Thank God for the protection
of His wings.

45 · *Grateful That God Provides for Me*

My God will supply all your needs according
to His riches in glory in Christ Jesus.
PHILIPPIANS 4:19

There was no food to feed the children. Nevertheless, George Müeller instructed the three hundred orphans to sit down in the dining room around the tables. He led them in a prayer thanking God for the food. Then they waited. George didn't know where the food would come from. But God had always faithfully provided. God had provided a building to house the orphans. He had provided caregivers, furniture, clothing, and food. Whenever George prayed about their needs, answers came. The money, supplies, or food often came at the last minute, but God had never let him down. And so they waited.

Within minutes, a baker knocked on the door with several batches of bread. Soon there was another knock. A milk cart had broken down in front of the orphanage. The milkman needed to dispose of the milk so he could fix the wheel. Could they, by any chance, make use of it? George smiled. There was just enough milk to meet the needs of the thirsty children.[17]

George was so confident that God would answer that he thanked God for the provision even before it arrived. Your needs may be different from the needs of those orphans. But you can be sure that God will supply all your needs too (Matthew 6:33). What do you need today? Why don't you follow George's example and thank God for the answer even before it arrives.

MEDITATION

When have you asked God about a need and seen Him provide? Why is it sometimes difficult to trust Him to provide? How can you rely on God to meet your current needs? How can you help meet the needs of others?

GROW GRATEFUL
Thank God that He richly provides for all your needs.

46 · Grateful That God Carries Me

In all their suffering, He suffered, and the Angel
of His Presence saved them. He redeemed them
because of His love and compassion.

Isaiah 63:9

The 1992 Summer Olympics will always stand out in my mind because
of one poignant event. Near the end of the men's four-hundred-meter
race, Derek Redmond, from Great Britain, collapsed, clutching his leg.
Officials moved toward Redmond to assist him off the track, but Derek
shouted them away. In excruciating pain, and with tears streaming
down his face, he struggled to his feet and began to slowly and ago-
nizingly inch down the lane. The crowd watched in stunned silence.

Suddenly, a stout, middle-aged man jumped out of the stands,
dashed past security officials, ran onto the track, and propped up the
injured runner. The man was Derek's father. Fighting off security, the

Redmonds moved toward the finish line together—the son leaned heavily, sobbing with pain, while the father, crying tears of his own, lent strong support and gentle words of encouragement.[18]

This touching story illustrates how our heavenly Father supports and carries us. As we read in today's verse, He lifted and carried the children of Israel on their difficult journey to the promised land. And what He did for them He will also do for you. When life gets tough and you feel as though you can't take another step, you can rely on the strong arms of your heavenly Father. He feels your pain. In love and compassion He will lift you up and carry you to the finish line.

MEDITATION

When were you hurting and needed God to carry you? How do you feel knowing that God suffers when you suffer? Why can you trust Him to carry you right to the end?

GROW GRATEFUL
Thank God for supporting
you to the finish line.

47 · *Grateful That God Delivers Me*

"I will deliver him; I will protect him because he knows My name. When he calls out to Me, I will answer him; I will be with him in trouble. I will rescue him and give him honor."
PSALM 91:14–15

SOS has been used as an emergency distress signal since the early 1900s. But what do the letters actually mean? They aren't an abbreviation for "Save Our Ship" or "Save Our Souls," as many people think. The letters mean absolutely nothing. They don't form any known word or abbreviation or acronym—and that's precisely why they were chosen. Seamen in distress needed a unique signal that would transmit clearly and quickly and would stand out from other telegraph transmissions. The sequence of triple dots and dashes was simple and elegant. It became the international favorite, for it could be sent quickly and easily and was hard to forget or misinterpret.

Vessels send out an SOS in hopes that someone will hear and respond to their distress call. Unfortunately, they can't always be certain that help will come. But God assures us that when we call out to Him, He will surely hear and answer. "The LORD will hear when I call to Him" (Psalm 4:3). He promises to faithfully rescue and deliver us from trouble. Isn't it good to know that whenever you hit rough waters you can send out a quick SOS to God? Your prayer doesn't need to be long or complicated. You don't even need to pray out loud. A silent *Help me, Lord* will suffice. When you call, He will deliver you. He will come to your aid and help you safely navigate the situation.

MEDITATION

Why do you think God doesn't always rescue us when and how we would like to be rescued? Why does this not negate the fact that He is with us and that He always answers our SOS?

GROW GRATEFUL
Thank God that He always answers your cry for help.

48 · *Grateful That God Helps Me*

> He Himself has said, I will never leave you or forsake
> you. Therefore, we may boldly say: The Lord is my
> helper; I will not be afraid. What can man do to me?
> HEBREWS 13:5–6

Have you ever posted a Help Wanted ad? My husband once posted an
ad for a clinical assistant that attracted more than one hundred and
fifty résumés. Of those, only three or four applicants appeared quali-
fied for the job. Brent interviewed them and hired the best one. But
after a couple of weeks, it became apparent that she couldn't handle
her work responsibilities, and he had to let her go. It's so hard to find
good help these days!

Are you as amazed as I am that God promises to help us? After a
great victory, the prophet Samuel erected a stone monument to com-
memorate God's help. He named the monument *Ebenezer*, which
means "the Stone of Help" (1 Samuel 7:12). The Old Testament frequently described God as a helper who comes to the aid of His people

(Psalms 10:14; 30:10; 54:4; 63:7). But Jesus promised that this help would become even more present, profound, and personal. The Father would send "another Helper, to be with you forever" (John 14:16 ESV).

The Helper (Greek: *parakletos*) is a distinctive title for the Holy Spirit, who was poured out on the day of Pentecost. He is the Spirit of Christ who resides in the heart of every true believer (Romans 8:9–11; Ephesians 1:13–14). This Helper is your ever-present source of counsel, instruction, guidance, discernment, gifting, enablement, comfort, transformation, strength, and power. You can be bold and brave, knowing that this Mighty Helper gives you all the help you need.

MEDITATION

How do you feel knowing that the Helper, the Holy Spirit, dwells with you? How can you make a habit of engaging His help more? Can you identify a way in which He has helped you recently?

GROW GRATEFUL
Thank God for ways in which the
Holy Spirit helps you.

49 · Grateful That God Equips Me

His divine power has given us everything required
for life and godliness through the knowledge of Him
who called us by His own glory and goodness.

2 PETER 1:3

After the sinking of the *Titanic* in the early 1900s, governments
established minimum safety standards in the construction, equipment,
and operation of boats. Federal law specifies the type of navigation system, communication system, distress system, lights, fire equipment,
life boats, and life jackets that various types of vessels must have on
board. Even if people are just paddling a canoe, it's mandatory that
they wear life jackets and carry a whistle or airhorn, a bailer, a throw-
able life ring, and a distress signal like a flare.

These minimum requirements, enforced by the US Coast Guard,
ensure that boaters will have everything they need to handle any circumstance they might encounter at sea.[19] If you were operating a boat
and encountered rough seas or some sort of other emergency, you'd

be extremely grateful to have the mandated equipment on hand. It's reassuring to know that when you reach for something you need to get you out of a tough situation, it will be there. Just as boats are equipped to handle circumstances at sea, so God's divine power equips us with everything required for *life* and everything required for *godliness*. Today's verse indicates that because we know Jesus, we do not lack anything necessary for success. God has put everything into our boats . . . *everything*!

Do you feel overwhelmed by life? Are you facing some rough, choppy waters? Regardless of your circumstances, rest assured that God has already provided you with the "equipment" to safely navigate through. You can be confident that His divine power has given you everything you need.

MEDITATION

If God's divine power has given us everything we need, why do we sometimes feel that we lack what we need? What situation are you currently facing for which you feel underequipped? How can you rely on God in this situation?

GROW GRATEFUL
Thank God that you have everything you need.

50 · Grateful That God Strengthens Me

> Be strengthened by the Lord and by His vast strength.
> EPHESIANS 6:10

Human strength is a fragile illusion. It often fails when we encounter difficult circumstances. Suddenly, out of the blue, life can fall apart. An accident. A grim diagnosis. The loss of a job. Calamity. Betrayal. Relationship breakdown. These are the times when we see how weak we really are.

The girl-power slogans on our T-shirts may advertise that we have GRL-Power, or that we are Pretty Smart. Pretty Tough. Pretty Awesome. Pretty Fierce. That Girls Can Do Anything, or that Strong Looks Good on Me. But deep down, we know it's not true. Our own strength is woefully inadequate. The slogans are hollow. No amount of personal empowerment can silence the nagging realization that we don't have what it takes without God.

We just don't.

Have you ever felt that way? I have. When I have reached the end of my capability and don't have an ounce of strength left to draw on, that's when the power of God becomes exceedingly precious to me. It's then that I cling to Him to receive what He has promised. "He gives strength to the weary and strengthens the powerless. Youths may faint and grow weary, and young men stumble and fall, but those who trust in the LORD will renew their strength; they will soar on wings like eagles; they will run and not grow weary; they will walk and not faint" (Isaiah 40:29–31).

When you have no strength left and there's nothing you can do but fall into the arms of your strong heavenly Father, you will find strength there.

MEDITATION

What does it mean to be strengthened by the Lord? How can you make a habit of drawing on His vast strength rather than your own? For what challenge do you need His strength today?

•   •   •   •   •   •   •   •

GROW GRATEFUL
Thank the Lord that He strengthens you.

51 · Grateful That God Removes Fear

> I sought the LORD, and He answered me and delivered me from all my fears. Those who look to Him are radiant with joy; their faces will never be ashamed.
>
> PSALM 34:4–5

Hannah Hurnard wrote *Hinds' Feet on High Places*, an allegory of a young woman named Much-Afraid. Much-Afraid, an orphan with deformities of her face and feet, lives with the Family of Fearlings. They live in the Village of Much-Trembling in the Valley of Humiliation. But one day she meets a Shepherd, who offers to give her feet like a deer to climb out of the deep valley and up to the High Places, where her blemishes would be washed away.

The Shepherd introduces Much-Afraid to Sorrow and Suffering, who will travel with her and help her on this journey. Though she is fearful, Much-Afraid chooses to trust the Shepherd. The path is fraught with dangers, but with the Shepherd's oversight, and Sorrow and Suffering's help, she finally makes it to the High Places. There, she is transformed and given a new name, Grace and Glory.

Her story is much like David's. David was fleeing for his life when he wrote Psalm 34. He felt much afraid. We all know what fear feels like. We fear many things. We fear failure and loss. We fear being judged, ridiculed, or rejected. We fear being abandoned and alone. We fear hurt, pain, and suffering. We fear the future and the unknown. Thankfully, the promise of deliverance for those who are fearful is more than a wishful fantasy. David upheld it as a reality for all who seek the Lord. The Lord delivers us from *all* our fears and replaces our anxiety with joy.

MEDITATION

What causes you anxiety? What do you fear? Why were Sorrow and Suffering the companions the Shepherd assigned to help Much-Afraid? According to David, what must you do to be delivered from fear?

GROW GRATEFUL
Thank God that He delivers you from fear.

52 · Grateful That God Makes Me Brave

> Be strong and courageous; don't be terrified or afraid
> of them. For it is the LORD your God who goes
> with you; He will not leave you or forsake you.
> DEUTERONOMY 31:6

Each day, after reporting on current events, newscasters usually end their broadcast with a feel-good story. And often it's a story of courage. Like the man who jumped into rushing floodwaters to rescue a dog. Or the teens who chased a carjacker to rescue two children. Or the hero who ran into the burning building while everyone else was running out. Stories like this give us the impression that courage involves a single brave act in the face of danger. But there's a less dramatic and more everyday type of courage that doesn't make the evening news. And people who have it are arguably even stronger and braver than those the media lauds as heroes.

The Bible indicates that courage is doing the right thing even when it's the hard thing. Courage is speaking up against the ungodly ideas pushed by your college professor when all the other students are nodding their heads. It's refusing to watch the X-rated show when all your friends are pressuring you to join in. It's enduring scorn and abuse on social media for your old-fashioned beliefs. It's refusing to return evil for evil when you are berated and slandered or mocked and ostracized. Courage stands strong even when it stands alone.

Today's verse provides the reason you can be brave in the face of opposition. It's because you're not really alone—"For it is the LORD your God who goes with you; He will not leave you or forsake you." He will make you brave.

MEDITATION

When was a time you had to stand against the crowd and do the right thing even though it was hard? How often does your fear of people keep you from being brave? What can you do the next time you're in a situation that requires courage?

GROW GRATEFUL

Thank God that He is with you to give you courage.

53 · *Grateful That God Gives Me Hope*

> Praise the God and Father of our Lord Jesus Christ. . . .
> He has given us a new birth into a living hope through
> the resurrection of Jesus Christ from the dead and into an
> inheritance that is imperishable, uncorrupted, and unfading.
> 1 PETER 1:3–4

Self-made millionaire Eugene Lang was asked to deliver the commencement address to the sixth graders at his old East Harlem elementary school. He intended to tell them that he had attended the same school, that through hard work he had made a lot of money and achieved success, and that if they worked hard, maybe they could become successful too. But when he looked out at the audience of underprivileged, ethnic-minority students, he knew the words would ring hollow. Statistically, most of them would never even finish school. He could not bring himself to hold out empty hope for achievements they would not have the tools or resources to attain.

So, on the spur of the moment, Lang made an outrageous promise.

If the sixth graders stayed in school, he would help finance their college education. Lang's promise infused that class of students with hope. They defied the school's astronomical dropout rate. Three-quarters of them graduated. More than half went to college.[20]

Hope is more than wishful thinking. Hope is confident expectation. When we hope in God, we are banking on a sure thing. Today's verse assures us that we can be certain of a rich inheritance. Just as the students' confidence in the millionaire's promise encouraged them to stay committed to their studies, so your confidence in God's promises can help you stay committed to living out your faith. When the going gets tough, hope in God will help you persevere.

MEDITATION

Is there a situation in your life that makes you feel helpless and hopeless? According to 1 Peter 1:3–4, why can you still have hope? How can you remain hopeful even when things appear hopeless?

GROW GRATEFUL
Thank God that He gives you a living hope.

54 · Grateful That God Helps Me Conquer

In all these things we are more than
conquerors through him who loved us.

ROMANS 8:37 ESV

The apostle Paul described Christians as "more than conquerors." The
Greek word for *conqueror* in today's verse literally means "super-
conqueror." The image that comes to mind is that of David conquering
Goliath. David was just a boy when he killed Goliath with a stone
from a sling. Goliath was a descendent of the Rephaim, a fierce race
of giants who were the original inhabitants of the land of Canaan.
The Rephaim were a formidable people. Most of the Israelites were
intimidated by their sheer size and strength, describing themselves as
"grasshoppers" in comparison (Numbers 13:33). David was the only
one who wasn't scared to take on the giant-sized problem of Goliath.

Why was David unafraid? Because he knew that God would give him strength to conquer. "He trains my hands for war so that my arms can bend a bow of bronze" (Psalm 18:34 ESV). David trusted God to give him "super" power to fight battles he couldn't possibly win on his own.

Scripture teaches that God can give all of us supernatural ability to face and conquer problems. Through hardships or pressures, heart-aches or distress, through tragedies or disasters, and even through persecution or martyrdom, *we are more than conquerors* through Jesus—we are super-conquerors! You may be facing some giant-sized problems. Just remember that God gives you strength to take on even the biggest problems. Your arms can bend a bow of bronze. In Jesus, you are a *super-conqueror* who can triumph over them all!

MEDITATION

Why do you think David had the courage to face one giant-sized problem after another? According to Romans 8:37, what makes us super-conquerors? What problem do you need to conquer today?

GROW GRATEFUL
Thank God that He helps you conquer.

55 · *Grateful That God Comes*

> Let the heavens be glad and the earth rejoice; let the sea and all that fills it resound. Let the fields and everything in them exult. Then all the trees of the forest will shout for joy before the LORD, for He is coming.
> PSALM 96:11–13

When my firstborn son, Clark, was about three years old, he would expectantly watch at the window for Daddy to come home from work. Each day, when the time drew near, he'd climb up on the easy chair in front of the window, part the sheers, rest his little chin on his hands and his elbows on the chair back, and steadfastly wait until he saw the car pull up. Then, with a shriek of excitement, he'd run to greet Daddy at the door.

This memory reminds me of how we ought to eagerly and expectantly wait for God. David, the psalmist, set a good example. He said, "I wait for the Lord more than watchmen for the morning" (Psalm 130:6). Just as watchmen were certain of the coming of dawn, and stayed alert, awaiting it, so David was certain that God would come every day. Not the "Big-C" coming of the Messiah's physical advent on earth, but the "little-c" comings that God weaves into the fabric of our daily lives.

God comes every day. In today's verse, we see that creation joyfully and excitedly welcomes His appearance. Do you? Do you expect God to come? Do you diligently watch for those moments when He speaks or tangibly makes His presence known? I hope so, because "His appearance is as sure as the dawn" (Hosea 6:3). So don't forget to watch for Him. In the hustle and bustle of your daily activity, stay expectant and alert. For He will certainly come.

MEDITATION

When was a time you saw God "show up" during your day? How diligently do you watch for Him to come? What could you do to increase your attentiveness and sense of expectation?

GROW GRATEFUL
Thank God that He comes to those who watch for Him.

56 · *Grateful That God Mends*

He heals the brokenhearted and binds up their wounds.
PSALM 147:3

David, the author of today's verse, endured many sorrows. He lost people he loved. He was betrayed by those he regarded as trusted and loyal friends. Even his own son conspired against him! But through the pain, David learned something important about God. Not only does God heal broken bodies—He also heals broken hearts.

The Hebrew word for "heal" means to sew together, to mend, to repair or refresh, to make sound or whole. The image that comes to my mind is a childhood memory of my mother skillfully mending socks. Mom would stretch the worn or gaping part of the sock over the back of her hand. Then, with a large-eyed needle and yarn, she'd quickly stitch back and forth between the edges, creating a parallel picket fence of yarn over the damaged area. Finally, she'd weave up and down across the pickets, filling in all the gaps with a neat, tight lattice of new material.

The German Reformer Martin Luther sometimes referred to God as *Herrn Gottes Flicker*, "Lord God Mender."[21] The image is apt. Our Lord is the mender of broken things. He mends sin, rottenness, hurt, failure, broken spirits, broken bodies, and broken hearts. Whenever our spirits are wounded, He is faithful to repair the damage. If your heart feels torn, spend some extra time with the Lord God Mender today. Give Him all the frayed and ripped pieces. Healing may be a process, but He will surely bind up your wounds and mend your broken heart.

MEDITATION

When has God mended your broken heart? Are there holes in your heart that currently need mending? Do you consistently turn to God to bind up your wounds and heal your broken heart? Why or why not?

GROW GRATEFUL
Thank God that He will mend your broken heart.

57 · *Grateful That God Makes the Crooked Straight*

> Every valley will be filled, and every mountain
> and hill will be made low; the crooked will
> become straight, the rough ways smooth.
>
> LUKE 3:5

Concrete walkways and driveways can sink and crack over time as the ground beneath them settles. This results in an uneven surface that creates a dangerous tripping hazard. Our driveway had reached that point. I constantly stumbled over the cracked, uneven surface between the driveway and sidewalk. I wanted to do something about it before someone took a bad fall. So I hired a mud jacking company to lift and level out the concrete slabs. They drilled several small holes through the surface. Then they pumped a thick mud mixture under the slab to put upward pressure on the sunken portion and slowly raise it back up to its original grade. After the repair, our driveway was level again. There was no more tripping. I was so relieved and grateful.

What that mud jacking company did for my driveway is what Jesus spiritually does for us. Sin creates dangerous cracks along the path. We trip over faulty words, attitudes, and actions. We hurt ourselves and others too. But God promises to make the crooked straight and the rough ways smooth. He repairs the cracks. His Spirit exerts upward pressure on the sunken areas of our lives to bring them up to grade. Are sinful words and attitudes tripping you up? Are cracks in your character causing you to fall? If so, you can address the problem by calling in the Expert. He will turn those rough places into level ground (Isaiah 42:16).

MEDITATION

What do you think it means for Jesus to fill the valleys, level the mountains, make the crooked straight and the rough ways smooth? Which rough path do you need Him to level for you today?

GROW GRATEFUL
Thank God that He makes the crooked straight.

58 · Grateful That God Secures My Steps

God—He clothes me with strength and makes
my way perfect. He makes my feet like the feet
of a deer and sets me securely on the heights.
PSALM 18:32–33

Radium Hot Springs is a popular vacation spot in the spectacular
Canadian Kootenay Mountains. My family has often enjoyed soaking in
Radium's hot, soothing mineral water and gazing up at the awe-inspiring
cliffs above. On one visit, we were treated to an astonishing spectacle.
A large, curly-horned bighorn sheep scaled down the steep vertical wall
beside the pool. He nimbly descended to about ten feet above us, where
he paused to nibble on something growing on the rock face. Everyone
in the pool stopped to gaze in wonder. How could he be so sure-footed?
That sheer, precipitous surface didn't have any apparent outcroppings
on which he could stand. We watched in fascination, wondering if he

would lose his footing and fall. But he didn't. After enjoying his snack, he agilely and gracefully clambered back up to the top.

Just as that bighorn sheep safely navigated the face of that treacherous cliff, so God will give you the strength to walk securely through the challenging parts of life. He doesn't always remove the precipice or eliminate the danger. But when the terrain is rocky, when the way seems treacherous, and when a fall appears imminent, He will secure your footing. When you feel as though you are emotionally clinging to the side of a cliff, ask God to provide you with a strong and sure foothold. He will make your feet like the feet of that bighorn sheep so you can securely walk on even the most challenging surface.

MEDITATION

When have you hit a rough patch in life and felt as though you were in danger of losing your footing? Why do you think God offers us deerlike feet instead of offering to simply eliminate the danger?

GROW GRATEFUL
Thank God that He
secures your steps.

59 · Grateful That God Corrects Me

> See how happy the man is God corrects; so do
> not reject the discipline of the Almighty.
> JOB 5:17

Have you ever had to work with a know-it-all who rejected input and correction? In college, my husband was part of a track-and-field relay team. At one point the team asked a sprinter to join them for an upcoming national competition. The sprinter was a champion runner, but he had never run a relay. Nevertheless, after only the first practice, he decided he knew everything there was to know about passing a baton. He didn't need any more input. Whenever the coach or one of the veterans tried to correct his technique, he bristled. He didn't appreciate their efforts to help.

At the track meet, the team ran extremely well and finished in first place. But their elation over winning was short-lived. The judge disqualified them because the know-it-all sprinter had made an illegal baton pass. His refusal to be corrected ultimately cost them the gold medal.

The best athletes are open to being coached. They understand that they need to heed correction in order to succeed. It's no different in the Christian life. We need God's correction. He gives us His Word to reprove, correct, and train us in righteousness (2 Timothy 3:16). We ought to be grateful for God's correction, because even though it may cause discomfort, it's extremely beneficial. "No discipline seems enjoyable at the time, but painful. Later on, however, it yields the fruit of peace and righteousness to those who have been trained by it" (Hebrews 12:11).

MEDITATION

Why is it often difficult to be corrected? How well do you accept correction? When have you seen the Word of God correct your behavior? In which way was this correction painful? In which way was it beneficial?

GROW GRATEFUL
Thank God for reproving, correcting, and training you.

60 · Grateful That God Speaks

> God spoke to the fathers by the prophets at
> different times and in different ways. In these
> last days, He has spoken to us by His Son.
> HEBREWS 1:1–2

Several months before his third birthday, my son Jonathan stopped talking. He stopped wanting to read books. He stopped running to answer the phone. He changed from a sweet, happy boy into a difficult and angry one. When he came into the kitchen one day, pointed to the cookie jar, and soundlessly moved his mouth, I knew that something was terribly wrong. A trip to the audiologist confirmed my worst fears. Jonathan's world had inexplicably gone silent. He was legally deaf. Thus began the long and painful journey of teaching him how to speak. Now Jonathan reads lips and speaks so well that his hearing impairment often goes unnoticed. But I'll never forget how dark and difficult those early days were.

Can you imagine what it would be like if God didn't speak to us? Or if we couldn't talk to Him? We wouldn't get to know Him. We wouldn't know what He thinks or feels. We wouldn't be able to develop a close relationship. Thankfully, God is neither deaf nor mute. He speaks and He listens. He spoke by the prophets at different times and in different ways. He spoke through His Son, Jesus. And He continues to speak through His creation, through His Word, and through His Holy Spirit. Have you been listening to the God who speaks? And have you been speaking to the God who listens? Don't neglect this important relationship. Take some time to listen today.

MEDITATION

According to Hebrews 1:1–2, what are some of the ways in which God has spoken? Why is the Bible such an important foundation for knowing what God has to say? How much effort do you put into listening to the God who speaks?

GROW GRATEFUL
Thank God for speaking
and for listening.

61 · Grateful for God's Word

> The instruction of the LORD is perfect, renewing one's
> life; the testimony of the LORD is trustworthy, making
> the inexperienced wise. The precepts of the LORD
> are right, making the heart glad. . . . The ordinances
> of the Lord are . . . more desirable than gold.
> PSALM 19:7–10

Open the drawer of your hotel room nightstand, and chances are you'll find a Gideon Bible. In 1908, a group of traveling Christian business-men made it their goal to put a Bible in every hotel room in the United States. Since then, the Gideons have placed more than two billion Bibles in hotels around the world. Before the practice was outlawed, they also distributed Gideon New Testaments in schools.

There's a small, worn, faded-red Gideon New Testament sitting on the shelf in my office. The cover is tattered and loose. The binding glue has disintegrated. The pages are falling out. But despite its poor condition, this New Testament is extremely precious. My husband received it when he was in fifth grade. Seven years passed before he read it. But when he did, it completely transformed his life.

The preface to the Gideon Bible says, "This Book reveals the mind of God . . . read it to be wise, believe it to be safe, practice it to be holy. It contains light to direct you, food to support you and comfort to cheer you. . . . Owned, it is riches; studied, it is wisdom; trusted, it is salvation; loved, it is character; and obeyed, it is power." Psalm 19 confirms that reading and meditating on the Word of God will nourish your spirit, equip your mind, and gladden your heart. Brent has experienced all of this to be true. I hope you have too.

MEDITATION

How did the author of today's verses feel about God's Word? If you desired God's instruction more than gold, how might that change how often you read your Bible? Which promised benefit in Psalm 19:7–10 is most attractive to you?

GROW GRATEFUL
Pray through today's verses,
praising God for His Word.

62 · Grateful That the Bible Is True

> The words of the LORD are pure words, like silver refined in an earthen furnace, purified seven times. You, LORD, will guard us; You will protect us from this generation forever.
> PSALM 12:6–7

In 1981, Janet Cooke won a Pulitzer Prize for a *Washington Post* article about an eight-year-old heroin addict named Jimmy. In 2014, a *Rolling Stone* magazine article described a gang rape by fraternity members as part of an initiation rite. In 2019, the public learned that actor Jussie Smollett was the target of a vicious hate crime. What do all these stories have in common? They were untrue. Cooke had to give back the Pulitzer Prize. *Rolling Stone* magazine had to retract the article and pay a hefty defamation settlement. Smollett faced lawsuits, community service, and public disgrace.

These days it's so hard to know what's true. News reports on one side of the political spectrum are contradicted by news reports on the other. It's obvious that the famous age-old question posed by Pilate at Jesus' trial is just as relevant now as then: "What is truth?" (John 18:38). Thankfully, we are not left without an answer.

Truth is what God says, and we can read that in the Bible. God's Word is "right and true" (Psalm 33:4 NIV), "perfect" (19:7), and "flawless" (18:30 NIV). Scripture is "the embodiment of knowledge and truth" (Romans 2:20 ESV). It is the standard for truth (John 17:17). The entirety of it is truth (Psalm 119:160). In a time when truth is so difficult to discern, you can trust the Bible. You can read it with confidence, knowing that God's Word is pure, holy, and true.

MEDITATION

What is truth? Why is it important to have a reliable, unchanging standard for truth? How can you tell whether you genuinely believe the Bible to be true? How can you rely on Scripture more as your source of truth?

GROW GRATEFUL
Thank God that His Word is true.

63 · Grateful That God Is My Shepherd

> The LORD is my shepherd; I shall not want. He makes me lie down in green pastures. He leads me beside still waters.
> PSALM 23:1–2 ESV

The metaphor of Shepherd and sheep is used more than two hundred times in Scripture to describe God's relationship to us. The comparison is apt. Sheep are social creatures with a mob mentality. They follow whoever appears to be the most prominent sheep in the group. They are also prone to wander off alone and get themselves into predicaments. They get lost, stuck, or injured. Or they get turned over on their backs and can't get themselves back on their feet. What's more, they don't have any natural means of protection from predators. Left to themselves, sheep cannot and will not last long. To survive—and to thrive—they need the constant care, protection, and guidance of a shepherd.

Today's verses are some of the most popular and beloved in the entire Bible. Perhaps you know them by heart. But have you ever taken the time to look past their familiarity and think deeply about what they say about God's care for you? God is *your* shepherd. There is nothing *you* lack. He makes *you* lie down in green pastures. He leads *you* beside still waters.

The metaphor was rich and powerful for David, the shepherd who wrote the psalm. You may be a city slicker who hasn't even seen a real live sheep. But that doesn't make the imagery any less profound for you. If you take the time to ponder it, I think you'll join him in exclaiming, "We, your people, the sheep of Your pasture, will thank You forever" (Psalm 79:13).

MEDITATION

When has the Lord made you lie down in green pastures? How does He lead you beside still waters? What else does Psalm 23 say about the ways in which He shepherds you? What do you need from your Shepherd today?

GROW GRATEFUL
Pray through Psalm 23, thanking
God for how He shepherds you.

64 · Grateful That God Is My Light

> Light dawns for the righteous, gladness
> for the upright in heart.
> PSALM 97:11

Our family has a rustic cabin in northern Alberta, far from the lights of the city. When I say "rustic" I mean no toilet and no running water (though we do have electricity). To do your business, you need to go to the outhouse that's situated in the bush behind the cabin. Once, I got up in the middle of the night to make the trek. Yikes! Power failure. No lights. I groped my way to the door through the inky darkness. Outside, the moon and stars were obscured by clouds. It was the blackest night I can remember. I slowly inched my way toward the outhouse, sliding my feet along the ground and keeping my arms extended to keep from walking face-first into a tree. (Or a bear!) Somehow I managed to accomplish my mission and make it safely back to bed. But it was an incredibly eerie experience. I was so thankful when the light finally dawned.

The Bible says that God is light and that people who know Him walk in the light. We don't need to stumble around in the dark like I did that weekend at the cabin. Though difficult circumstances can darken our paths, we can trust Him to illuminate the next step. Today, if your path seems dark, and you can't see which way to go, I encourage you to draw near to God and wait on Him. The night won't last forever. He promises that light (and gladness) will surely dawn.

MEDITATION

When have you physically stumbled around in the dark? Spiritually, when we walk through dark valleys, how can we ensure we have enough light? In what situation would you like more of God's light today?

GROW GRATEFUL
Thank God that He
is your light.

65 · Grateful That God Is My Stronghold

The LORD is my rock, my fortress, and my deliverer,
my God, my mountain where I seek refuge, my shield
and the horn of my salvation, my stronghold.
PSALM 18:2

David was in deep trouble. His father-in-law, King Saul, was trying to kill him. It was clear that David wouldn't be safe in the urban centers of Israel. There was only one thing to do—head for the hills! So he fled to the Judean mountains near the Philistine border. It was an ideal place to hide. The limestone rock was honeycombed with numerous caverns. Here, he and his men took refuge in the cave of Adullam. The word *Adullam* means "refuge" or "resting place." The Stronghold of Adullam provided David a measure of physical safety and rest, but even more secure was the spiritual refuge in which he took cover. David didn't just hide in the cave; he also hid himself in God.

David's psalms are peppered with references of God as a stronghold, rock, fortress, and refuge. Many of them were written when he was in danger and on the run. Yet even after he was king and safe within the walls of the palace, David continued to run to God for refuge whenever he was in emotional turmoil. Where do you turn when you feel worried, stressed, or afraid? Many people take refuge in the mall, in a glass of wine, or on social media. But there's an infinitely more secure and comforting place to hide. Whenever you feel emotionally unsettled, you can figuratively head for the hills and take shelter in God. He is the stronghold in which you can find comfort and rest.

MEDITATION

What does it mean to make God your stronghold? Is He the first place you run when you feel worry, stress, doubt, or fear? For what circumstance do you currently need to head for the hills and take shelter in God?

GROW GRATEFUL
Pray Psalm 18:2 as a
prayer of gratitude.

66 · Grateful That God Is My Everlasting Rock

> You will keep the mind that is dependent on You in perfect peace, for it is trusting in You. Trust in the LORD forever, because in Yah, the LORD, is an everlasting rock!
> ISAIAH 26:2–4

The lighthouse of Alexandria was one of the seven wonders of the ancient world. Equivalent to a forty-floor skyscraper and covered in gleaming white marble, it soared even higher than the great pyramids of Egypt. For many centuries it was one of the tallest man-made structures on earth. The architect understood that in order to support a structure that big, he needed to design an incredibly solid foundation. So he had the builders dig down deep through the topsoil to the underlying rock. On the rock, they laid massive blocks of granite, joined together with molten lead. His design became the archetype for the construction of all tall buildings.

In New Testament times, the lighthouse of Alexandria was a famed tourist attraction that had stood securely for hundreds of years. It's possible that Jesus had the foundation of this monumental structure in mind when He said that everyone who hears and obeys His words is like a wise man who builds his house on the rock (Matthew 7:25). Just as the foundation of the lighthouse enabled it to withstand storms and tidal waves, so will building your life on God make you strong. With Him as your rock, you won't be shaken. He will keep your mind and emotions from being tossed about. Even when the rains fall, and the floods come, and the winds blow, He will keep your heart strong and steady and your mind in perfect peace.

MEDITATION

What does it mean to build your life on the Everlasting Rock? When has this foundation kept your mind at peace during a difficult time? How can you always keep your mind at perfect peace?

GROW GRATEFUL
Thank God that He
is your Rock.

67 · Grateful That I Can Trust God

> When I am afraid, I will trust in You. In God, whose word I praise, in God I trust; I will not fear.
>
> PSALM 56:3–4

Erik Weihenmayer was the first blind person to climb to the top of the highest peak on each of the seven continents. To make it to the top, he had to listen carefully to the little bell tied to the back of the climber in front of him so he would know which way to go. He also needed to listen to the instructions of his guide. On Everest, they wore special throat microphones and ear plugs so they could communicate while wearing oxygen masks. According to Erik, the greatest fear in climbing blind was in the reaching.[22] He felt most afraid when he had to let go of his secure perch and reach for what he could not see. His level of success was directly related to his willingness to let go and trust his guide.

Can you imagine how difficult it would be to climb a mountain if you were unable to see? But often that's exactly what difficult circumstances force us to do. Perhaps you are facing a daunting health battle, or a relationship breakdown, or a financial struggle, or some other significant heartache or loss. You can't see what's ahead. You feel as if you're on a treacherous cliff and climbing blind. Take comfort in the fact that though you can't see what's coming, God can. He is an expert guide. Though you are afraid, you can trust Him to direct you to the next handhold and guide you safely to the top.

MEDITATION

What things do you fear? Looking back over your faith journey, can you identify some instances where God faithfully guided your steps? In what area is He currently asking you to let go, reach out, and trust?

GROW GRATEFUL
Thank God that He is a
trustworthy guide.

68 · *Grateful That God Is by My Side*

> With You I can attack a barrier, and with
> my God I can leap over a wall.
> PSALM 18:29

Have you seen the movie Ice Castles? It tells the story of Lexie Winston, a world-class figure skater and promising Olympic contender. Tragedy strikes when Lexie falls and hits her head on the ice. The freak accident leaves her virtually blind. Though she can see only light and blurry shapes, her boyfriend spurs her on to get back on skates and pursue her dreams. With his support, she overcomes her fears and limitations to compete once again.

Reviewers called the 1978 drama a "schmaltzy classic skating movie for romantics."[23] I was so enamored with the theme song that I sang it to my husband at our wedding. The lyrics captured my sentiments exactly. I had faith that even if Brent and I faced storms, together we'd find some light. Because Brent was with me, I'd be alright.

Okay. Maybe the song was just as sappy as the movie. But the point is an important one. Our ability to face a challenge is affected by whom we face that challenge with. The author of today's verse was able to attack barriers and leap over walls. He knew that with God by his side he could accomplish far more than he could accomplish alone. What about you? Do you confidently face challenges, or do you shy away from them? Think about a challenge you are currently facing. You can trust God to help you conquer it. He'll help you attack the barrier and leap the wall. With Him by your side, you'll be alright.

MEDITATION

Is there someone in your life whose support increases your confidence to face a challenge? Why does God's presence increase our confidence? Which barrier do you currently need the courage to tackle?

GROW GRATEFUL
Thank God that He
is by your side.

69 · *Grateful That God Is Enough*

Who do I have in heaven but You? And I desire nothing on earth but You. My flesh and my heart may fail, but God is the strength of my heart, my portion forever.
Psalm 73:25–26

There wasn't enough food for refugees in post–World War II Germany. And even when there was, the Allies withheld it. Desperate for food, my mother and her family scoured the forest for mushrooms and berries and anything else they could eat. They did get food rationing cards every two months, for which they could claim their allotted portion of bread, cheese, eggs, meat, sugar, and canned goods. But the portions were meager. One small pat of butter every week, for example. *If* butter was even available. Having a ration card didn't guarantee that you would get something to eat.

In today's verse, David called God his "portion." A portion is an individual's part or share. In calling God his portion, David indicated that he was aware that God was everything his hungry heart desired.

Unlike the portions my mother and other refugees received, God is enough. In fact, He is more than enough. "You satisfy me," David declared, "as with rich food" (Psalm 63:5).

Many of us don't know what to do about our unfulfilled longings. We chase after success, riches, material goods, fame, beauty, pleasure, sex, and romance—thinking these things will satisfy. But ultimately, they are never enough. God is the only portion big enough to fill the hungry human heart. If you are wise, you will seek satisfaction in God rather than in things that will not satisfy. Like David, you will choose to make God your portion forever.

MEDITATION

Do you feel a void in your life? To what are you turning to fill this void? How can you make God the strength of your heart and your portion forever? Why is He enough?

GROW GRATEFUL
Thank God that He is enough.

70 · Grateful That God Is for Me

> The LORD is for me; I will not be afraid.
> What can man do to me?
> PSALM 118:6

When our family plays board games, everyone is out to win. It's a no-holds-barred, every-man-for-himself, dog-eat-dog rivalry. Through our sons' teen years, we often played Settlers of Catan. The battles were epic. Still, they were all in good fun. Mostly. But things took a turn for the worse when we expanded the game with cards that could be used as a method of attacking other players. This (and the ambiguous rules) started to create problems. Competitions turned into arguments and hard feelings. Some players felt that others really were "against them." Things got so bad that we had to call it quits and find some board games that were less combative.

It's one thing to have an opponent in a game—but having a real-life opponent is an entirely different matter. Especially when that opponent is out to do you harm. Some people think God is out to do them harm. Perhaps they've lost a job or encountered a series of unfortunate events. They look at the hand they've been dealt and conclude that God is not on their side. But according to the Bible, this is not true. The Lord is for you and not against you. He may not always answer your prayers in the way you expect. Nevertheless, He delights in your well-being (Psalm 35:27) and rejoices in doing you good (Jeremiah 32:41). Whenever life gets rough or people try to do you harm, don't despair or be afraid. Remember that God is always on your side.

MEDITATION

How do you feel knowing that God is for you and not against you? Why do people sometimes struggle to believe that God is for them? What difference does it make to have God on your side when people come against you?

GROW GRATEFUL
Thank God that He is for you.

71 · Grateful That God Makes a Way

> "Look, I am about to do something new; even now it is coming. Do you not see it? Indeed, I will make a way in the wilderness, rivers in the desert."
>
> ISAIAH 43:19

In the classic Broadway musical and film *The Sound of Music*, the Reverend Mother sends Maria away from the convent to work as a nanny for the Von Trapp family. Maria is unsettled at the idea of leaving the abbey and giving up on her dream of becoming a nun. The Reverend Mother reassures her with the now-famous cliché, "When the Lord closes a door, somewhere He opens a window." In other words, whenever one opportunity ends, another opportunity will come along—and it will probably be a better one. Sure enough, the closing abbey door leads to the opening of the window that ushers Fräulein Maria into the arms of the dashing Captain Von Trapp.

Though the cliché is meant to help people stay positive in the face of disappointment, it isn't exactly true. God doesn't promise that when something doesn't work out, something better is waiting for us just around the corner. His pledge is far more substantive than that. He promises to sustain us amid life's disappointments. When all the doors and windows remain shut, He helps us make our way through the dark room, and He sustains us. Our circumstances do not always change for the better. But we can be confident that He will use them to change *us* for the better. "'I know the plans I have for you'—this is the LORD's declaration—'plans for your welfare, not for disaster, to give you a future and a hope'" (Jeremiah 29:11).

MEDITATION

When was the last time you faced a closed door? During this time, how did God make a way in the wilderness and rivers in the desert? Why can you trust Him with closed doors, even when there are no windows in sight?

GROW GRATEFUL
Thank God that He makes a way through the wilderness.

72 · *Grateful and Peaceful*

> Let the peace of the Messiah . . . control
> your hearts. Be thankful.
> COLOSSIANS 3:15

Some things just go together. Like salt and pepper. Peanut butter and jam. Or lightning and thunder. Where you find one, you almost certainly find the other. Colossians 3:15 indicates that peace and gratitude are coupled like that. Gratitude tags along with peace. And peace tags along with gratitude. If you see one, you'll probably see the other too, because they are intertwined and interdependent.

When you think about it, the pairing makes sense. Feeling agitated and distressed usually causes us to complain and grumble. Our lack of peace contributes to our lack of gratitude. But it also works in the other direction. Our lack of gratitude contributes to our lack of peace. When we complain and grumble, it adds to our agitation and distress.

Paul urged the Colossian believers to let the peace of Christ control their hearts. In Greek the word *control* literally means "to sit as umpire." An umpire makes the calls. He rules the game. Paul was saying that just as an umpire makes calls about the plays of a game, so we should let God's peace be the umpire that rules and controls the impulses of our hearts. Whenever we begin to feel agitated and distressed, we can allow God's peace to overrule that play. But how? "Be thankful" is how. Paul likely added the command to be thankful because he understood the symbiotic relationship between peace and gratitude. More gratitude leads to more peace. So be thankful.

MEDITATION

What do you think it means to allow the peace of Christ to sit as umpire over your heart? When was a time you let Him overrule your agitation and distress? How do you think gratitude contributes to peace?

GROW GRATEFUL
Thank God for His peace.

73 · *Grateful for a Quiet Harbor*

They rejoiced when the waves grew quiet. Then
He guided them to the harbor they longed for.
PSALM 107:30

Brent and I were vacationing in Huatulco, Mexico, a popular place for
Canadians to escape the cold and snow of winter. The centerpiece of
Huatulco's charm is the *Bahias de Huatulco*, nine bays that are shel-
tered from the winds, waves, and ocean currents. Because of this, they
boast miles of golden, sandy beaches and warm, calm, crystal-clear
water. One day as we were snorkeling, we noticed a sudden influx of
birds and boats into the bay. We had no idea why they were all con-
gregating. Someone explained that it was because of the lunar eclipse
that would take place that night. The eclipse would trigger extremely
strong ocean tides. A storm was forecast to follow. The boats—and
the birds—had come into the bay seeking calm waters.

I don't know about you, but I often long for calm waters. When
I struggle to find an empty slot on my calendar, when the messages

come in faster than I can answer, when the needs are greater than my capacity, I am grateful there is a place to escape the frenzy. As the old hymn says, "There is a place of quiet rest, near to the heart of God." When life gets busy and you're feeling frenetic and overwhelmed, it's important to set aside your cell phone and carve out just a few moments to spend alone with the Lord. He will calm the waves and guide you to the peaceful harbor you long for.

MEDITATION

When life gets busy and frenetic, where do you normally turn to find some quiet rest? What are some reasons people often turn to God only as a last resort? How can you make God your harbor on a daily basis?

GROW GRATEFUL
Thank God that He provides
a quiet, safe harbor.

74 · *Grateful for a Glorious Kingdom*

> All You have made will thank You, LORD; the
> godly will praise You. They will speak of the glory
> of Your kingdom and will declare Your might.
> PSALM 145:10–11

An estimated three billion people (give or take half a million) tuned in to watch the 2011 wedding between Prince William and Kate Middleton. Seven years later, the wedding of Prince Harry and Meghan Markle attracted roughly the same number of viewers.[24] That means that almost half the people on earth watched the young royals get married! The thought is staggering. Especially since the United Kingdom is home to less than 1 percent of the world's total population.

Interest in the royal family obviously isn't restricted to the queen's subjects. People everywhere are fascinated with them. We pay attention almost despite ourselves. We talk about Kate's newly designed garden. Or about Meghan's post-baby workout routine. We discuss their latest outfits and share news about their relationships and activities. And the media helps feed the frenzy. Hardly a day goes by without another photo or story about the royals.

Psalm 145:10–11 indicates that godly people talk about God's kingdom just as enthusiastically as royal watchers talk about the House of Windsor. God's loyal subjects tell people how splendid and magnificent their Great King is. They speak about His realm and His reign and His majesty. They excitedly share information about His Royal Highness's family. They can't keep it to themselves. Notice that today's verse links the attitude of gratitude with the act of testifying. *Thanksgiving* and *praise* are expressed through *speaking* and *declaring*. If we don't talk about the kingdom, then we're probably not thankful for it. If we're truly thankful, *we will speak of the glory of God's kingdom and will declare His might.*

MEDITATION

How is God's kingdom more glorious than the House of Windsor's? Why does an attitude of gratitude inevitably show up in our speech? What does your speech indicate about the level of gratitude in your heart?

GROW GRATEFUL

Tell God what you admire about His kingdom.

75 · *Grateful for an Unshakable Kingdom*

> Let us be grateful for receiving a kingdom that
> cannot be shaken, and thus let us offer to God
> acceptable worship, with reverence and awe.
> HEBREWS 12:28 ESV

It's been years since the magnitude-9 earthquake shook Japan, triggering a catastrophic tsunami and nuclear disaster. The quake was the biggest ever recorded in the nation's history and among the most powerful ever recorded in the world. Can you imagine how frightened the people felt when the ground started to violently shake and buildings started to collapse? But feelings of fear and panic aren't restricted to natural disasters like earthquakes. Those feelings can be triggered whenever we feel the ground beneath our feet metaphorically begin to shift.

Hebrews was written to a group of believers who felt shaken when they were persecuted for their faith. Many had lost their homes, livelihoods, and family relationships. What's more, they could tell the persecution was getting worse. The tremors were getting more violent and they were feeling increasingly anxious and fearful. The writer of Hebrews assured them that regardless of how badly they might get tossed about, they could draw strength and comfort from the fact that God's kingdom could never be shaken.

Perhaps you are feeling apprehensive about tremors taking place in your life. Maybe you're experiencing a significant shift in a relationship, in your finances, in your living situation, or in your or a loved one's health. Regardless of how bad the upheaval may get, remember that you remain on sure footing with God. You can stand firm and bravely endure the quake, for you are a part of the kingdom that cannot be shaken.

MEDITATION

When have you sensed your life was being shaken? How did the instability and uncertainty make you feel? How can faith in God's unshakable kingdom stabilize us during times of upheaval?

GROW GRATEFUL

Thank God that His kingdom is unshakable.

76 · Grateful for My Heavenly Citizenship

> You are no longer foreigners and strangers, but fellow
> citizens with the saints, and members of God's household.
> EPHESIANS 2:19

My mother wore her best dress the day my parents got their Canadian
citizenship. They nervously rode the bus downtown. There, in a
wood-paneled courtroom, they stood before a black-robed, white-
wigged judge. With hands on a Bible, Mom and Dad solemnly swore
an oath of allegiance. The judge asked them to sign some papers
renouncing their fealty to Germany, and more papers confirming
their oath to their new country. Then, with a rap of his gavel, he
pronounced them citizens of Canada. He declared that they would
henceforth be entitled to all the rights and privileges and subject
to all the responsibilities, obligations, and duties of a Canadian
citizen. Then he came down from the bench, handed them their

official papers, shook their hands, and on behalf of the government of Canada, officially welcomed them.

From that day on, we were no longer foreigners and strangers. We were fellow citizens. We were so happy to finally have a country to call our own! Yet over the years, my father often reminded me that as Christians, we are foreigners and strangers on earth. Given my family's history as postwar refugees, the reminder is especially poignant. I am grateful to Canada for taking us in. But I'm even more grateful for an eternal citizenship. As blessed as we all are to be citizens of great countries like Canada and the United States, we should never lose sight of the fact that we are just passing through. Our citizenship is in heaven. That's our hearts' true home.

MEDITATION

What does it mean to be a citizen of heaven? Which citizenship has a greater pull on you—your earthly or heavenly one? How can you be a good citizen of heaven while you still live on earth?

GROW GRATEFUL
Thank God that He made you
a citizen of heaven.

77 · *Grateful That God Makes Me Thrive*

> The righteous thrive like a palm tree and grow like a cedar tree in Lebanon. Planted in the house of the Lord, they thrive in the courts of our God. They will still bear fruit in old age, healthy and green.
> PSALM 92:12–14

The Holy Land is called "the land of the palms." A date palm grows to forty, fifty, even eighty feet tall. The trunk fibers are extremely elastic, so the tree bends but does not break with the force of the wind. Palms begin to bear fruit about six years after being planted and produce more than three hundred pounds of dates each year. A palm continues to be productive for more than a century, and as the tree grows older, the fruit gets sweeter and more abundant. When Psalm 92 says that we will *thrive like palms*, it means that over time we will grow increasingly fruitful and strong.

A person who loves God also *grows like a cedar tree in Lebanon,* today's verse says. The mountains in Lebanon were famous for their cedar forests, which were called "the glory of Lebanon." The cedar is a magnificent, deep-rooted evergreen tree that grows for as many as two thousand years. It can reach enormous diameters and heights. Its fragrant wood is red in color and is especially durable and resistant to decay. It was highly esteemed for its beauty.

When you walk with God, you will flourish like these two magnificent trees! Over time you will grow stronger, more resilient, more beautiful, and more fruitful. Don't be discouraged if you feel like that's not happening. Growth is a process. If you keep your roots planted in Christ, you will surely grow. And thrive! Even in old age you will remain healthy and green.

MEDITATION

What do you think it means to be planted in the house of the Lord? What growth have you seen in your life? Would you characterize your spiritual life as healthy, green, and fruitful? If not, what do you need to do to stimulate some growth?

GROW GRATEFUL

Thank God that He makes you thrive.

78 · *Grateful in All Circumstances*

> Give thanks in all circumstances; for this is
> the will of God in Christ Jesus for you.
> 1 Thessalonians 5:18 esv

Today's scripture is an important verse about gratitude. When we looked at this verse previously, we focused on the second part of the verse, the part that tells us *why* we ought to grow grateful. It's because gratitude is God's will for us. Giving thanks is a spiritual discipline that's an essential part of our relationship with Him. It's the process through which we habitually recognize God's greatness and acknowledge Him as the One through whom all blessings flow.

We're looking at this verse again because it not only explains *why* we ought to be grateful but also tells us *when* we ought to be grateful. We are to give thanks in all circumstances. All circumstances? What about difficult circumstances like a car accident or cancer diagnosis?

What about the devastating heartbreak of a wayward child or divorce? What about natural disasters and loss? And what about the sheer evil of heinous crimes committed against innocent victims? It seems ludicrous that God would ask us to be thankful for things like this.

It's important to note that God doesn't say to give thanks *for* all circumstances; He tells us to give thanks *in* them. There's a big difference. We thank God even in times of difficulty and evil—even during the deepest, darkest trial—because our hope remains. "We know that all things work together for the good of those who love God: those who are called according to His purpose" (Romans 8:28). That's why we can give thanks.

MEDITATION

What's the difference between being grateful *for* difficult circumstances versus being grateful *in* them? How might gratitude in hard times affect a person's attitude and perspective? In what current difficulty do you need to exercise more gratitude?

GROW GRATEFUL
Thank God that you
can have hope.

79 · Grateful When I Don't Feel Grateful

Whatever you do, in word or in deed, do everything in the name of the Lord Jesus, giving thanks to God the Father through Him.

COLOSSIANS 3:17

Have you ever heard of the Feeling Wheel? It's a useful chart developed by Dr. Gloria Willcox in the early 1980s to help people identify and better describe their emotions. Six core emotions are located at the center of the wheel—sad, mad, and scared, which are negative emotions, and joyful, powerful, and peaceful, which are positive ones. A secondary ring of words helps narrow these feelings down. For example, someone who feels mad can choose a more specific descriptor, such as hurt, hostile, angry, or critical to describe the way they are feeling. A third, outer ring gets even more specific. In all, there are seventy-two adjectives to help people pinpoint the specific emotions they're experiencing at any given point in time.

Thankfulness is located on the positive side of the Feeling Wheel, under the broad category of peaceful feelings. It's directly opposite the scared feelings category, which includes descriptors such as confused, anxious, and overwhelmed. When we feel negative scary emotions, or when we feel mad—snarky, irritated, or perturbed—we generally don't feel thankful. In fact, the wheel indicates that thankful is probably the last thing we feel. Nevertheless, Colossians 3:17 instructs us to give thanks in *whatever we do, in word or in deed . . .* in *everything*! The directive encompasses every area of our lives—including our emotions. God wants us to give thanks even when we don't feel particularly thankful and even when our emotions are pulling us in the exact opposite direction.

MEDITATION

How can you give thanks when your emotions are pulling you in the opposite direction? What will likely happen to your emotions if you stop to give thanks? Why is it important for you to learn to give thanks in whatever you do?

GROW GRATEFUL

Next time you feel a negative emotion, stop and give thanks.

80 · Grateful Even for Weakness

> He said to me, "My grace is sufficient for you,
> for power is perfected in weakness." . . . So I take
> pleasure in weaknesses, insults, catastrophes,
> persecutions, and in pressures, because of Christ.
> For when I am weak, then I am strong.
>
> 2 CORINTHIANS 12:9–10

On a hot July afternoon, a diving accident transformed Joni Eareckson Tada's life forever. She went from an active teenager to a quadriplegic confined to a wheelchair. Now, more than fifty years later, it's astonishing to see what Joni has accomplished. She has authored more than fifty books, is an advocate for disabled persons, and has affected millions of people's lives worldwide. And she has done all this while living with quadriplegia, cancer, and chronic excruciating pain.

Joni claims that her quadriplegia is her greatest asset because it forces her into the arms of Jesus every morning. "Deny your weakness," says Joni, "and you will never realize God's strength in you. . . .

The weaker I am, the harder I must lean on God's grace; the harder I lean on him, the stronger I discover him to be, and the bolder my testimony to his grace."[25]

The apostle Paul said the same sort of thing. He was grateful for weakness—not because he enjoyed being weak but because it allowed God to show Himself strong. Human inability puts God's ability on display. When you don't have what it takes and must rely on God, He gets the greater glory. So embrace your weakness. Lean hard on God for the power to do what you do not have the strength for. The harder you lean, the stronger you will find Him to be.

MEDITATION

When have you experienced God to be strong in your weakness? How did your inability put God's ability on display? Can you be grateful for a weakness and at the same time desire to be delivered from it?

GROW GRATEFUL
Thank God that when you are weak, He is strong.

81 · *Grateful Even When Bad Gets Worse*

> Though the fig tree does not bud and there is no fruit on the vines, though the olive crop fails and the fields produce no food, though there are no sheep in the pen and no cattle in the stalls, yet . . . I will rejoice in the God of my salvation!
>
> HABAKKUK 3:17–18

Habakkuk described a series of escalating problems. First, the fig tree didn't blossom. That meant no figs. Figs served as a delicacy, so losing them was more of an annoyance than anything else. Next, there was no fruit on the vines. Grapes were used to produce the common daily beverage in the country, so that posed a major inconvenience. Losing the olive crop, however, significantly hampered their ability to function. They'd have no oil for cooking or lighting lamps. Even more critical would be the loss of grain. That would mean starvation for large segments of the population. The final blow would be the loss of the livestock, as this would deprive them not only of food but also of their ability to produce it.

Regardless of how bad it got, Habakkuk was determined to "rejoice in God." That is, he was determined to focus on the bigness of God rather than the bigness of the problem. Even in the most horrible bad-to-worse situation, Habakkuk knew that God would be faithful to see him through.

It's not easy to be grateful when we face a tough situation. It's even tougher to be grateful when things go from bad to worse. And when the problems pile up and seemingly have no end, that's when it's the most difficult. It's also the time when we need gratitude the most. When you face an ever-worsening crisis, do what Habakkuk did. Don't focus on the bigness of the problem. Rejoice in the greatness of God instead.

MEDITATION

When have you faced a time when the problems piled up and things went from bad to worse? What was your response? How can you "triumph in Yahweh" during such times (v. 18)? Why can you trust Him to see you through?

GROW GRATEFUL

Thank God that you can triumph even when bad gets worse.

82 · *Grateful for Times of Reprieve*

> Blessed are those whose strength is in you, in whose heart are the highways to Zion. As they go through the Valley of Baca they make it a place of springs; the early rain also covers it with pools. They go from strength to strength; each one appears before God in Zion.
>
> PSALM 84:5–7 ESV

Today's passage talks about pilgrims who were making the trip to Jerusalem. Historically, Jews traveled there three times a year to celebrate the great feasts of Passover, Pentecost, and Tabernacles. The phrase "in whose heart are the highways to Zion" simply means they had their hearts set on going. They were eager to make it to the Holy City for the celebration. But it wasn't an easy trip, especially since they had to pass through the Valley of Baca.

The word *Baca* is derived from the verb "to drip." It's the name of a shrub that grows in arid conditions and drips sap profusely when it's cut. Because of this imagery, the ancients referred to the Valley of Baca as the "Valley of Weeping." Baca was a hot, dry, waterless place—and difficult to traverse. Only occasionally, during the rainy season, did small pools form and provide the parched ground, and weary travelers, any reprieve.

You can probably tell that these verses have a figurative as well as literal meaning. Figuratively, they speak of our journey through life to our heavenly home. The road can be tough. But God will replenish us along the way. As we make our way through the Valley of Weeping, we will experience times of respite from the harsh, dry terrain. We'll go from pool to pool—from strength to strength—until the happy day we appear before God in the heavenly city of New Jerusalem.

MEDITATION

Why does God figuratively lead us from pool to pool rather than through an oasis? Are you currently resting beside a pool or fighting against the blistering, dry heat? How do you feel, knowing you will encounter more pools along the way?

GROW GRATEFUL
Thank God for times of reprieve.

83 · *Grateful for Rest*

> LORD, You are my portion and my cup of
> blessing. . . . Therefore my heart is glad and my
> spirit rejoices; my body also rests securely.
> PSALM 16:4–10

Most people extol the benefits of a vacation, yet researchers were alarmed to discover that in the year leading up to their study, more than half of Americans (56 percent) didn't take a break.[26] That's concerning, they say, because failing to take breaks from work can be seriously bad for our health. Those who forego times of R&R have higher blood pressure, don't sleep as well, and have higher levels of stress.

Rest is a prominent theme in the Bible. After six days of creation, God rested from work on the seventh day. And He instructed the Jews to follow this example. Every week they were to observe a Sabbath day. The Hebrew word (*sabat*) means to rest or cease from labor. Rest is a break from work that provides a time for mental and spiritual restoration. But the concept goes beyond taking a day off or going on vacation.

The Bible also speaks of another kind of rest. Christians, by faith in Christ, enter into rest (Hebrews 12:22–24). All who come to Him stop striving and find rest—relief, release, peace, and satisfaction—for their souls. What's more, the spiritual rest we now experience in Jesus points to the time when all earthly struggle and striving will cease, and we will fully experience God's rest.

Are you feeling tired and overwhelmed? Jesus said, "Come to Me, all of you who are weary and burdened, and I will give you rest" (Matthew 11:28).

MEDITATION

How do you think your work and rest patterns are affecting your well-being? What does the discipline of seeking physical rest teach us about spiritual rest? What do you need to do in order to experience more of both kinds of rest?

GROW GRATEFUL
Thank God that He gives
rest to the weary.

84 · *Grateful to Be Replenished*

> Satisfy us in the morning with Your faithful love so
> that we may shout with joy and be glad all our days.
> PSALM 90:14

Exercise can stress muscles and damage individual muscle fibers.
Drinking a cup of chocolate milk can help replenish exhausted, damaged muscles and significantly reduce recovery time. Recent research
by scientists at Central Washington University discovered that chocolate milk replenishes muscles even more effectively than pricey,
high-performance sports drinks.[27] Choosing the right post-workout
drink is just one part of the equation, however. Not only is it important *what* an athlete uses to refuel her muscles; *when* she does it is just
as important. Sports performance trainers say that it's important to
drink the chocolate milk within thirty to sixty minutes of working
out, as that's when muscle glycogen (energy) stores are at their lowest.[28]

It's crucial to replenish our weary bodies. It's even more crucial
to replenish our weary souls. Drinking in God's love helps us recover

from the damage this sinful world inflicts. It relieves our sadness and sorrow, our emotional aches and pains, our anxieties, our fears, and everything that stresses and drains our spirits. We are refueled, re-energized, renewed.

The psalmist made a habit of meeting with God early each morning: "I rise before dawn and cry out for help; I put my hope in Your word" (Psalm 119:147). "I call to You for help, Lord; in the morning my prayer meets You" (Psalm 88:13). Morning or night, as you make a habit of meeting with God, He'll satisfy you with His faithful love and fill you with joy and gladness.

MEDITATION

Where do you feel the stress and damage that life has inflicted on your soul? Take a moment to drink in the love of God and allow it to mend and replenish you. Express your gratitude for the ways in which He refuels, re-energizes, and renews your soul.

GROW GRATEFUL
Thank God that He replenishes and satisfies you.

85 · Grateful That Sad Can Become Glad

> You turned my lament into dancing; You removed my sackcloth and clothed me with gladness, so that I can sing to You and not be silent. LORD my God, I will praise You forever.
> PSALM 30:11–12

In the classic 1936 novel Gone with the Wind, the widowed young Scarlett does a fair amount of hand-wringing about how long she ought to wear black. The custom at the time was for widows to wear nothing but black for a year or more following a spouse's death. Grieving widows also refrained from attending parties. But Scarlett was done with grief. She accepted an invitation to dance and transitioned out of mourning clothes by donning a feathered, emerald-green bonnet. The change in color signaled that her time of mourning was over.

People in the Old Testament also wore black garments whenever they wanted to publicly express their grief and distress. The garments were made of sackcloth, an inexpensive, coarse material made from black goat hair. Someone wearing sackcloth wouldn't attend festivities. It was only when their time of lament was over that they'd take off their sackcloth, put on regular clothes, and again engage in normal daily activities.

David used this cultural practice as an analogy to describe the profound impact God has on our hearts and attitudes. God turns lamenting into dancing. Whether we're facing an aggravation, frustration, disappointment, or even deep sadness and grief, He alleviates our sorrows, worries, and cares. When you feel emotionally down, God can help with those heavy feelings. He can transform your sad to glad. He can remove the black sackcloth and clothe you in color so you can stop lamenting and start to dance.

MEDITATION

Over what situation or problem are you currently lamenting? What destructive, negative emotions do you feel? How can you focus on God instead of the problem and allow Him to take away your worries and cares?

GROW GRATEFUL
Thank God that He turns lament into dancing.

86 · *Grateful for a Happy Ending*

> You who are now hungry are blessed, because
> you will be filled. You who now weep are
> blessed, because you will laugh.
> LUKE 6:21

And they lived happily ever after . . .

Moviegoers love happy endings. Tragedies simply don't fare well at the box office. Audiences generally don't want to lay down their hard-earned cash to watch a depressing story. They don't want realism; they want a healthy dose of escapism. They want the ending with the perfectly choreographed kiss. The sky exploding with fireworks. Or the hero driving off into the sunset. The ending can be poignant and can make them shed a tear a two, but ultimately they just want to walk away with a warm, fuzzy feeling and a smile. The guy gets the girl. The foe is vanquished. The battle is won.

The reason we want movies to have happily-ever-after endings is because that's how we want our own real-life stories to end. We know that all too often they don't. The prince morphs into a toad. The dream turns into a nightmare. The win is accompanied by a terrible loss. We thought we were headed for happily ever after, but the plot takes an unexpected twist and becomes a tragedy instead. And the disappointment, pain, and heartache are profound.

One of God's most precious promises is that we can trust Him to write a happy ending to our story. Regardless of how painful and difficult life gets, we are guaranteed that for those who love Him, things will ultimately end well. He will wipe away every tear. Grief, crying, and pain will no longer exist (Revelation 21:4). In heaven, we will all get the happily-ever-after ending for which we yearn.

MEDITATION

When has your story taken an unexpected and disappointing turn? In what way does God write a happy ending even amid tragic and difficult circumstances? Why can you trust Him to do this for you?

GROW GRATEFUL
Thank God that He is writing a happy ending.

87 · *Grateful for Spiritual Blessings*

> Praise the God and Father of our Lord Jesus
> Christ, who has blessed us in Christ with
> every spiritual blessing in the heavens.
> EPHESIANS 1:3

I heard a story about a boy whose grandmother promised him that he'd get a special gift for his birthday. He imagined that she'd get him an action figure, a skateboard, a shiny bike, a video game, or one of the other items he'd written down on his list. When he ripped opened Grandma's box, all he found inside was a card and an envelope containing a few papers. "Stock certificates," she explained. He gave her an obligatory hug and mumbled his thanks. But he was keenly disappointed. It wasn't at all what he expected. The toys his friends gave him were so much better!

The boy stuffed the gift from Grandma into his desk drawer. Years later, as he was packing for college, he found the forgotten envelope.

To his utter shock and amazement, he discovered that the stocks were worth nearly a million dollars! Though he had shrugged it off as the lesser gift, Grandma had, in fact, given him the better one. Her gift far eclipsed the value of all those toys he had long discarded.

We are often like that boy. We overvalue temporal blessings like material possessions or food or clothing. And we undervalue spiritual blessings like redemption, forgiveness, and God's abiding presence and strength. Just imagine. God has blessed you with "every spiritual blessing in the heavens." His gift to you is infinitely greater than you can even fathom. Don't fail to appreciate its value or express your gratitude.

MEDITATION

Do you ask God for temporal blessings more than you thank Him for spiritual ones? Why do we tend to value the temporal over the spiritual? Make a list of all the spiritual blessings you receive.

GROW GRATEFUL
Thank God for blessing you with every spiritual blessing!

88 · Grateful for a Great Inheritance

I pray that the perception of your mind may be enlightened so you may know what is the hope of His calling, what are the glorious riches of His inheritance among the saints.
EPHESIANS 1:18

Hetty Green's father left her a $6 million inheritance. Over the course of her lifetime it grew to $100 million. By the time of her death in 1896, she was said to be the richest woman in the world. But she lived the life of a miserly pauper. She refused to spend a penny of her great inheritance. She wouldn't even spend the money on necessities. Hetty wore the same black dress every day. She used newspapers pulled from trashcans as undergarments. In order to save on her fuel bill, she refused to heat her tenement apartment or even cook her meals. She ate mostly dry oatmeal. When her son, Edward, aged nine, was run over by a wagon and injured a leg, Hetty refused to call a doctor, who would charge her money. Instead, she took the boy to several free clinics. Eventually the boy's leg had to be amputated.[29]

What a sad story. Though Hetty had the rights to all that money, she refused to spend it, and struggled along, trying to manage on her own meager resources. Yet how often do we spiritually do the same? Our heavenly Father bequeaths us an unfathomable supply of power, strength, peace, comfort, joy, and other riches. But often, instead of accessing that wealth, we struggle along on our own. Paul wanted his friends to dip into their wealth in Christ. He prayed that they would come to understand the extent of their glorious inheritance. I pray the same for you.

MEDITATION

Why do Christians fail to access the riches they have in Christ Jesus? How can you avoid making this mistake? What resources do you need from your heavenly Father today?

GROW GRATEFUL
Thank God that you share in His rich inheritance.

89 *Grateful for the Reward*

> The wicked man earns an empty wage, but the
> one who sows righteousness, a true reward.
>
> PROVERBS 11:18

A healthy-eating deli called Freshii recently opened next door to the fitness facility I attend. This casual-dining brand sells various fast and nutritious salads, soups, and wraps. It also sells delicious fresh-squeezed juices and smoothies. I decided that a delectable smoothie would be the perfect way to reward myself for consistently working out. So I started a reward system, which I've dubbed "Freshii Fridays."

The system works like this: At the beginning of each week I set some fitness goals. If, by Friday, I've reached those goals, I reward myself by going for a treat. Last Friday I enjoyed a Freshii green smoothie. This Friday I won't get anything because I skipped out on Monday's scheduled class. (Sigh.) Even though I knew I had already forfeited the smoothie, I worked out faithfully for the rest of the week. Why? Because ultimately, it's not the Freshii Friday reward that motivates me to exercise. As Emerson said, "The reward of a thing well done is having done it." But still, there's something extremely satisfying about getting a reward. The reward may not be the goal of the work, but it certainly is its crowning joy.

The Bible is chock-full of unblushing promises about the rewards that God will give to those who are faithful. So don't become weary of doing good. One day, a day even better than Freshii Friday *will* come. God will say, "Well done, good and faithful servant" and give you a fabulous reward (Luke 19:17 NIV).

MEDITATION

Have you ever received a reward for work you've accomplished? What part did the reward play in motivating you to stay committed? How do you feel knowing that righteousness will certainly be rewarded?

GROW GRATEFUL
Thank God that He rewards those
who sow righteousness.

90 · Grateful for a Greater Joy

> You have put more joy in my
> heart than they have when their
> grain and new wine abound.
> PSALM 4:7

Most countries observe Thanksgiving or another holiday in autumn to celebrate harvest. The Jews celebrated Sukkoth, which was also known as the Feast of Tabernacles or Festival of Booths. Lasting eight days, it was the longest and most festive Jewish holiday and, arguably, its most important.

Sukkoth was a fall festival that celebrated harvest and the abundance of God's blessing. But it was also a memorial of God's provision and protection of His people in the wilderness when they lived in tents on their way to the promised land. While other Jewish festivals included emotions of awe, repentance, and somber remembrance, the Torah commanded that Sukkoth be celebrated with pure joy (Deuteronomy 16:14). Essentially it was a massive, weeklong party that engendered such joy that it was celebrated with daily feasts and night-long dancing and singing.

In today's verse, David noted that God put more joy in his heart than the most bountiful harvest—and the most boisterous harvest celebration. His point was that the happiness people feel over material goods and earthly achievements can't compare to the happiness we find in God. Whatever it is that brings people joy, God gives us *more joy* than that! What brings you joy? A festive Christmas get-together? An evening out with your sweetheart? Buying a new home? A promotion at work? An exotic vacation? A big accomplishment? Whatever it is, I hope you can say, with David, that God gives you even *more joy* than that!

MEDITATION

When was an occasion you celebrated a happy accomplishment? What do you think of David's concept that God puts even *more joy* in our hearts than that? How can you tap into this joy?

GROW GRATEFUL
Thank God that He fills your heart with greater joy.

91 · *Grateful for Unending Joy*

> The redeemed of the LORD will return and come to Zion with singing, crowned with unending joy. Joy and gladness will overtake them, and sorrow and sighing will flee.
> ISAIAH 35:10

Two important ceremonies took place during Sukkoth, the Jewish Festival of Tabernacles. The first was the nightly illumination of the temple. Priests lit the great fires, enormous candelabras whose towering flames burned all night, reminding the Jews of the pillar of fire that guided them in the wilderness. The lamps were said to be so bright that they lit up the entire city. Priests read Scriptures about the true "Light"—the promised Messiah of God, who would someday dwell (tabernacle) among them (Isaiah 9:2). Then the music and night-long festivities would begin.

The party continued until daybreak the next morning, when the second ceremony took place. Priests led a parade down to the Pool of Siloam to fill a golden pitcher with "living water" and ceremonially pour it out as a petitionary act, both for rain and for the promised living water of the Messiah. How beautifully appropriate, then, that Jesus cried out at the festival, "If anyone is thirsty, he should come to Me and drink!" (John 7:37–38).

No wonder Sukkoth was such a joyful occasion! It prophetically pointed to the coming of Jesus. What's more, it also points to the time when our earthly wanderings will end. One day we will gather in the New Jerusalem. Joy and gladness will overtake us, and we will be crowned with unending joy. Unending joy! Let that sink in. No sadness. No tears. No crying. Only unending joy. And all the joy you have ever experienced on earth will pale in comparison.

MEDITATION

Why do you think the Jews were commanded to celebrate the festival of Sukkot with joy? What does it mean to have living water flow from deep within? Why will we be "crowned with unending joy"?

GROW GRATEFUL
Thank God for crowning you with unending joy.

92 · Grateful Hallelujah

> May Yahweh, the God of Israel, be praised from everlasting to everlasting. Let all the people say, "Amen!" Hallelujah!
> PSALM 106:48

One word that's been used extensively in the church's worship and liturgy since early times is *Hallelujah. Hallelujah* is the English transliteration of a Hebrew phrase. The first part, *hallelu*, means "praise ye." The final syllable, *jah*, is a shortened version of God's name, Yahweh. Thus, "Hallelujah" literally means, "Praise Ye Yahweh!" Essentially, it's a command to give God thanks. This call to worship seems to have been used by priests in the temple to signal the opening and closing of a liturgical reading. The term occurs twenty-four times in the book of Psalms and usually falls at the beginning or end of the psalm. The ten psalms that open with "Hallelujah!" are commonly referred to as the Hallelujah Psalms.

The Jews continued the practice of using "Hallelujah" as a liturgical call to worship after they were dispersed from Jerusalem. By New

Testament times, however, "Hallelujah" seems to have become less of a formal call to worship and more of a spontaneous cry of praise and thanksgiving. The book of Revelation depicts the heavenly chorus joyfully singing, "Hallelujah!" (19:1–6).

Regardless of whether the word is used in formal worship or spontaneous praise, it clearly indicates that we ought to be grateful. Hopefully this book has helped you with that. Every day, as you thanked God in prayer, you were essentially saying, "Hallelujah!" And I hope you continue to offer up grateful hallelujahs for the rest of your life.

MEDITATION

When a priest said, "Hallelujah," what was he telling the congregation to do? Is it possible to say "Hallelujah" with your lips but fail to say it with your life? How can you ensure that your life says "Hallelujah" too?

GROW GRATEFUL
Pray Psalm 106:48 as a
hallelujah to God.

93 · Grateful Speech

> Through Him then, let us continually offer up
> a sacrifice of praise to God, that is, the fruit
> of lips that give thanks to His name.
> HEBREWS 13:15 NASB

There are some things that just don't belong together. Like a gold ring in a pig's snout (Proverbs 11:22). Or a pair of Jimmy Choo heels in a field of cow dung. Or a crystal wine goblet in a doghouse. If we want to truly honor God and give Him thanks, it's inappropriate for us to let ugly, unattractive speech remain in our vocabulary. "Coarse and foolish talking or crude joking are not suitable, but rather giving thanks" (Ephesians 5:4). Growing in gratitude doesn't simply involve saying more *thankful* things. It also involves saying fewer *unthankful* things. Grateful speech and ungrateful speech do not belong together. Tongues that bless God shouldn't curse those made in God's image. Blessing and cursing should not come out of the same mouth (James 3:10).

The writer of Hebrews encourages us to continually offer up a "sacrifice of praise" to God. His contemporaries would have been acquainted with the Old Testament practice of bringing a freewill offering to the temple to express thanks to God. If someone was grateful, he or she would bring an animal sacrifice and unleavened bread and cakes (Leviticus 7:12–13). This old way of thanking God has been replaced. Now, instead of the fruit of the farm, God wants us to offer up the good fruit of our lips. We are to express our gratitude through holy, transformed speech. And not only speech that explicitly thanks and blesses God but also speech that thanks and blesses the people around us.

MEDITATION

How does speaking kindly and respectfully to others also bless God? In what ways do our words reflect the condition of our hearts? How clean and holy is your speech? In what areas do you need to improve?

GROW GRATEFUL
Ask God to help you get rid of ungrateful speech.

94 · Grateful Prayer

> Devote yourselves to prayer; stay alert
> in it with thanksgiving.
> COLOSSIANS 4:2

The Bible encourages us to devote ourselves to prayer. This comes as no surprise. But did you notice that the Lord wants our prayers to be offered *with thanksgiving*? Whenever we pray, we are to do so with an attitude of gratitude. This is the case even when we're feeling anxious about a stressful situation and are petitioning God for relief. "Don't worry about anything, but in everything, through prayer and petition with thanksgiving, let your requests be made known to God" (Philippians 4:6). There it is again: prayer and petition *with thanksgiving*. The pattern is consistent. We are to pray with an attitude of gratitude. Thankfulness is apparently the backdrop for good praying.

So how does someone facing a messy situation, like divorce, pray with thanksgiving? It seems ridiculous to thank God for something that isn't good and that clearly doesn't make us—or Him—happy.

What do we thank Him for when life is going awry? Simple. We thank God for who He is and how He upholds us through our suffering and sees us through the mess. We thank Him for meeting our needs. We thank Him that He is in control. We focus our thanksgiving on His goodness and grace.

When we make a point of giving thanks, it forces us to take our focus off the bigness of the problem and to place it squarely on the bigness of God. Mixing thanks with prayer changes our prayers. Or, perhaps I should say, it changes us. That's why God wants us to pray with thanksgiving.

MEDITATION

On a scale of one to ten, with one being "never" and ten being "always," how frequently do you mix your prayers of petition with thanksgiving? How does giving thanks help address the problem of worry and anxiety?

GROW GRATEFUL
Make a request of God with thanksgiving.

95 · Grateful Song

> Let the message about the Messiah dwell richly among you, teaching and admonishing one another in all wisdom, and singing psalms, hymns, and spiritual songs, with gratitude in your hearts to God.
>
> COLOSSIANS 3:16

Singing is good for you. And researchers have been hard at work trying to explain why.[30] They've discovered that singing releases endorphins, a hormone associated with feelings of pleasure. A second chemical released during singing is oxytocin, which has been found to alleviate anxiety and stress. Singing requires you to breathe deeply. That draws more oxygen into your blood and improves your circulation, which also reduces stress.[31] What's more, study after study has found that the benefits of singing are compounded when people sing in a group.[32]

Singing soothes nerves, elevates spirits, and contributes to a person's sense of well-being. It's good for your emotions and your health. When you sing with others, it increases the benefits and the enjoyment. And even people who can't sing well will reap the rewards.[33]

Paul instructed his friends to sing psalms, hymns, and spiritual songs together with gratitude in their hearts to God. He didn't know that singing releases endorphins and oxytocin and increases blood oxygenation. Nevertheless, he was convinced that singing praises to God ought to be a common practice in the Christian community. For those who have experienced God's goodness, joyful singing is a natural and proper response. And so is gratitude.

Notice that Paul linked the attitude to the action. The words and melodies that come from our mouths should bubble up from the gratitude that resides in our hearts. This uniquely Christian type of singing not only blesses us—it also blesses God.

MEDITATION

How does singing affect your emotions? When you worship with other believers, how full do you sense your heart is with gratitude? How would more gratitude affect the way you sing?

GROW GRATEFUL
Sing a worship song with gratitude.

96 · Grateful Legacy

> We, Your people, the sheep of Your pasture,
> will thank You forever; we will declare Your
> praise to generation after generation.
> PSALM 79:13

I recently went over to my parents' home for lunch. As usual, we bowed our heads before the meal as my dad gave thanks. His entire prayer was laced with thanksgiving. Not only thanks for the food but also thanks for me and my visit, thanks for God's protection, for God's help and guidance, and for God faithfully providing everything we need, including an eternal home in heaven.

My parents are tremendous examples of thankfulness. At ninety-four and ninety-one years old, their bodies are starting to fail. Yet I have never heard them complain—not when they tell me about a challenging issue they are facing, nor when they are in extreme physical pain. Even then, they exhibit an attitude of gratitude. They'll say something like, "It hurts. But I'm so thankful God is with me."

I think of the conversation I had with my mom when, at eighty years old, she received a diagnosis of ovarian cancer. "Mary, don't you worry. God was faithful to me when we fled for our lives from Poland and when we were homeless refugees. He was faithful when we immigrated and didn't have any money for groceries. God has always been faithful. He's not going to stop being faithful now."

My parents learned how to be thankful in everything. Their attitude of gratitude has affected me profoundly. And I want to make sure I pass this legacy on to my children and children's children. Like them, declaring His praise "to generation after generation!"

MEDITATION

Is your family legacy one of gratitude or complaining? Which of your family or friends has exhibited an attitude of gratitude? How can you faithfully declare His praise to the next generation?

GROW GRATEFUL
Tell a younger person about what
God has done for you.

97 · *Grateful to Overflowing*

As you have received Christ Jesus the
Lord, walk in Him . . . just as you were
taught, overflowing with gratitude.
COLOSSIANS 2:6–7

Several years ago, shoppers at the Westfield Shopping Centre in London, England, were wowed by a whimsical thirty-foot-tall chocolate fountain. The Joyville Magnificent Musical Chocolate Fountain was part of a marketing campaign by international confectioner Cadbury. Inspired by *Willy Wonka and the Chocolate Factory*, the wacky purple contraption whirred and buzzed and played bright, carnival-like music. Twenty metric tons of bubbling, gurgling, molten chocolate circulated up through a swirly network of pipes, spilled over the top, and cascaded down to the mezzanine below. Wide-eyed children were welcomed to Joyville by purple-clad attendants, who took them on a tour of the massive gimmick. At the end of the tour, the children were treated to mouth-watering samples of Joyville chocolate.

The image of the Cadbury fountain bubbling over with chocolatey joy illustrates what God wants to see happen in our lives on a spiritual level. According to today's verse, we ought to "overflow" with gratitude. The Greek word means to exceed, be present in superabundance, and prove to be extremely rich. The verse indicates that this sweet, superabundant, overflowing joy is a by-product of having received Christ Jesus and of walking in Him. It doesn't happen without some effort on our part. Notice the words "just as you were taught." We need to learn how to follow Christ. We also need to learn how to overflow with gratitude.

MEDITATION

What is the connection between walking in Christ and overflowing with gratitude? On a scale of one to ten (with one meaning none and ten meaning overflowing), how much gratitude is bubbling up in your life? How can you increase the flow today?

GROW GRATEFUL
Thank God that walking in Christ
causes gratitude to overflow.

98 · *Grateful with All My Heart*

I will thank Yahweh with all my heart; I
will declare all Your wonderful works.
PSALM 9:1

Have you ever felt unappreciated? Perhaps you sent someone money, or
gave a gift, or perhaps you fixed, served, or did something special, but
instead of gratitude you received no response. No acknowledgment.
No thank-you. Nothing. All you heard were crickets. Or even worse,
you received criticism as a response.

I once voluntarily took on a lengthy project to serve some people.
It cost me an enormous amount of energy, time, and money. I received
no help. And though the people clearly benefited from my work and
made good use of what I had labored so hard to achieve, they never
expressed any thanks. All I heard was negative remarks about things
they didn't like. I felt disappointed, hurt, and unappreciated. What's
more, I had to fight against the inclination to become angry and resent-
ful. I could handle their lack of investment and participation. After

all, I volunteered for the task, and I gave without strings attached. But their lack of gratitude stung deeply. It hurt a lot.

You've likely felt unappreciated at some point in time. You gave freely, but the recipient's lack of gratitude felt like the gift was being thrown back in your face. I suspect that God feels the same way when we fail to be grateful for His generous gifts. Let's not be like the nine lepers who took Jesus' gift of healing and ran. Let's be careful to be like the one who returned to give Him thanks (Luke 17:11–19).

MEDITATION

When was a time you felt unappreciated? What difference would a word of thanks have made? How frequently do you express thanks to God for the ways in which He blesses you? What can you thank Him for today?

GROW GRATEFUL
Thank God with all your heart
for what He has done.

99 · Grateful Forever and Ever

> There was a vast multitude from every nation, tribe, people, and language, which no one could number, standing before the throne and before the Lamb . . . and they fell facedown before the throne and worshiped God, saying: "Amen! Blessing and glory and wisdom and thanksgiving and honor and power and strength be to our God forever and ever. Amen."
>
> REVELATION 7:9–12

Did you happen to attend the concert dubbed *the greatest show on earth*? Rock band U2's 360° concert tour that took place from 2009 to 2011 shattered records and left its mark on history. Not only was it the most technologically innovative, largest, and most expensive concert stage the world has ever seen, it was also the highest-grossing tour ever; taken in by more than seven million people. The enormous circular stage consisted of a two-hundred-ton metal behemoth of four arches nicknamed "The Claw." They soared more than fifteen stories high and formed a sci-fi type cathedral with a rotating platform, moving walkways, a monstrous speaker system, massive light rigs, and a huge central conical video display. Concertgoers were wowed by the spectacular display. They jumped, danced, cheered, and boisterously sang along with the famous band.

As impressive as the U2 tour was, it ended. And it's just a matter of time before it fades from memory and is upstaged by another *greatest show on earth*. But there's a festive gathering in heaven that will not end. It will be more dazzling and magnificent than any earthly production ever could be. A vast, countless multitude from every nation, tribe, people, and language will join the host of angelic beings around the throne of God in joyful, boisterous worship. It's good that we aim to grow grateful now, because when we make it to that otherworldly concert, we will praise and thank God forever and ever.

MEDITATION

How does growing grateful prepare us for heaven? In which ways have you grown more grateful through pondering the Meditations in this book? What do you need to do in order to continue growing grateful?

GROW GRATEFUL
Thank God for helping you grow more grateful.

100 · Grateful Throng

> You have come to Mount Zion, to the city of
> the living God (the heavenly Jerusalem), to
> myriads of angels in festive gathering.
> HEBREWS 12:22

The president of the United States is commander-in-chief of about half a million army personnel. This is more than the Russian army (320,000) but less than the Chinese, which, at upward of 1.5 million, is the largest army in the world.[34] But these numbers don't even come close to the heavenly forces that operate under God's command, including heavenly beings such as cherubim, seraphim, and armies of angels. Today's verse informs us that there are "myriads" of angels in heaven. Elsewhere, we are told the heavenly hosts number "countless thousands, plus thousands of thousands" (Revelation 5:11).

"Myriads" (tens of thousands) and "thousands of thousands" are not formulas or equations that literally indicate a specific quantity. These phrases are symbolic. They represent an immeasurably large number. The hosts of heaven "cannot be counted" (Jeremiah 33:22). The Lord is commander-in-chief of an army that is more numerous and more powerful than any other. Angels are real, beautiful, and powerful, but God sits enthroned above them all. They are His army, His ministers, His servants.

The Bible indicates that the host of angelic beings encircling God's throne praise Him night and day. They continually extol His virtues and give Him thanks. Did you notice how the writer of Hebrews described the scene? Theirs is a *festive gathering*! They are exuberant! They can't contain themselves. They are endlessly appreciative of who God is and what He does. It's good that you learn how to praise God now, for in heaven you will join their happy, grateful throng.

MEDITATION

When have you witnessed a festive gathering, and what was the reason for it? Why are the angels in heaven happy? What is the connection between their gratitude (praise and thanksgiving) and their joy?

GROW GRATEFUL
Thank God that you will join heaven's grateful throng.

101 · *Grateful Always for Everything*

> Giving thanks always for everything to God the
> Father in the name of our Lord Jesus Christ.
> EPHESIANS 5:20

I hope this book has convinced you that gratitude is supposed to be a way of life for Christians. And I hope that as you've worked your way through the Meditations, you've seen yourself become a more grateful—and happy, peaceful, and contented—person. The Bible indicates that we can be grateful in the brightest day and through the darkest night. We can give thanks whether we're standing on the highest emotional mountaintop or trudging through the lowest emotional valley. Thanksgiving can fill our hearts whether our circumstances bring us pleasure or pain, joy or sorrow.

Ephesians 5:20 sums it up well. It encourages us to give thanks "always for everything" to God the Father in the name of Jesus. The verse is a powerful reminder. And for me, it's a necessary one. Often, being grumpy seems far easier than being grateful. That's why I printed off a reminder to hang as a motto over my desk:

GIVE THANKS ALWAYS FOR EVERYTHING!

You might want to display this phrase from Ephesians 5:20 in a prominent place in your home or workplace too. Remember, Christian gratitude is more than warm, fuzzy feelings of appreciation for the good things we experience. Gratitude is a lifestyle—a hard-fought, grace-filled, Spirit-enabled discipline that takes the spotlight off *self* and gives thanks to God *always* for *everything*.

MEDITATION

How is it possible to give God thanks always for everything? What can you do to help you remember to give thanks? In which aspect of your life do you need to work harder to make gratitude part of your lifestyle?

GROW GRATEFUL
Today, give thanks always for everything.

Notes

1. Lauren Suval, "The Relationship Between Happiness and Gratitude," *Psych Central*, July 8, 2018, https://psychcentral.com/blog/the-relationship-between-happiness-and-gratitude/.

2. Mani Vaya, "The How of Happiness by Dr. Sonja Lyubomirsky, Book Summary," Book Summaries, October 14, 2017, https://www.2000books.com/wp/happiness-sonja-lyubomirsky/.

3. Elisabeth Elliot, *Love Has a Price Tag* (Ann Arbor, MI: Servant Publications, 1990), 97.

4. Sonja Lyubomirsky, "Eight Ways Gratitude Boosts Happiness," Gratefulness.org, accessed August 18, 2019, https://gratefulness.org/resource/eight-ways/.

5. "Lost for Words at the Grand Canyon, Arizona," Rough Guides, January 23, 2014, https://www.roughguides.com/article/lost-for-words-at-the-grand-canyon-arizona/.

6. The expression *mysterium tremendum et fascinans* is a Latin phrase first introduced by Rudolf Otto in 1923. See "Rudolf Otto's Concept of the 'Numinous,'" Kenyon College website, https://www2.kenyon.edu/Depts/Religion/Fac/Adler/Reln101/Otto.htm.

7. http://www.wilderdom.com/intelligence/IQWhatScoresMean.html.

8. David Mathis, "In and Out, in a Blaise of Glory," Desiring God, June 19, 2013, https://www.desiringgod.org/articles/in-and-out-in-a-blaise-of-glory.

9. "Two Florida Teens Swept Out into the Ocean Rescued by Boat Named 'Amen,'" *NBC News*, May 3, 2019, https://www.nbcnews.com/news/us-news /two-teens-stranded-ocean-prayed-help-then-along-came-boat-n1001576.

10. Walter A. Elwell and Philip Wesley Comfort, *Tyndale Bible Dictionary* (Wheaton, IL: Tyndale House, 2001), 1114.

11. Esther Landhuis, "Neuroscience: Big Brain, Big Data," *Scientific American*, January 26, 2017, https://www.scientificamerican.com/page/about-scientific -american/.

12. The National Science Foundation, quoted in Fran Simone, "Negative Self-Talk: Don't Let It Overwhelm You," *Psychology Today*, December 4, 2017, https://www.psychologytoday.com/blog/family-affair/201712/negative-self -talk-dont-let-it-overwhelm-you.

13. Portions of this devotion were taken from my book *The Right Kind of Strong* (Nashville: Thomas Nelson, 2019).

14. Adapted from "Sermon Illustrations," Sermonillustrations.com, http://www .sermonillustrations.com/a-z/f/father.htm.

15. Karyn Hall, "An Epidemic of Loneliness," *Psychology Today*, May 11, 2018, https://www.psychologytoday.com/ca/blog/pieces-mind/201805/epidemic -loneliness.

16. Mary A. Kassian, *Knowing God by Name: A Personal Encounter*" (Nashville, TN: LifeWay, 2008), 44. See also Spiros Zodhiates, *The Complete Word Study Dictionary: New Testament* (Chattanooga, TN: AMG, 2000).

17. George Mueller, "Orphanages Built by Prayer," Christianity.com, https://

www.christianity.com/church/church-history/church-history-for-kids/george
-mueller-orphanages-built-by-prayer-11634869.html.

18. Colin Ward-Henniger, "Olympics Moment: Derek Redmond Finishes 400M with Dad in Barcelona," CBSnews.com, August 4, 2016, https://www.cbsnews.com/news/olympics-moment-derek-redmond-finishes-400m-dad-barcelona/.

19. George Day, "Coast Guard Requirements: Safety Standards Set by the Pros," Boats.com, https://www.boats.com/coast-guard-requirements/.

20. Emily Langer, "Millionaire Who Financed College Dreams Dies at 98," *Washington Post*, April 11, 2017, https://www.washingtonpost.com/national/eugene-lang-millionaire-who-financed-college-dreams-dies-at-98/2017/04/11/7b5b6374–1dfa-11e7-ad74–3a742a6e93a7_story.html?noredirect=on

21. Heather Boerner, "Ice Castles Movie Review," Commonsensemedia.org, https://www.commonsensemedia.org/movie-reviews/ice-castles.

22. Erik Weihenmayer, *Touch the Top of the World: A Blind Man's Journey to Climb Farther Than the Eye Can See* (New York: Dutton, Penguin Random House, 2001). See also Claire Marshall, "How the First Blind Man to Summit Mount Everest Changed My Perspective on Fear," Huffpost.com, May 25, 2017, https://www.huffpost.com/entry/how-the-first-blind-man-to-summit-mount-everest-changed_b_59161939e4b02d6199b2ef04.

23. Heather Boerner, "Ice Castles Movie Review," Commonsensemedia.org, https://www.commonsensemedia.org/movie-reviews/ice-castles.

24. Sarah Lyall, "Royal Wedding Draws in Billions for a Day," Nytimes.com, April 29, 2011, https://www.nytimes.com/2011/04/30/world/europe/30britain.html?_r=1.

25. Joni Eareckson Tada, *God's Hand in Our Hardship* (Peabody, MA: Rose, 2012).

26. Christine Digangi, "56% of Americans Haven't Taken a Vacation in a Year," *Money*, August 17, 2015, http://money.com/money/4000332/take-a-vacation-now/.

27. "Train, Drink Milk, Repeat" *GTHL Canada*, November 15, 2017, http://www.gthlcanada.com/article/train-drink-milk-repeat.

28. Kelly L. Phillips, "Exactly Why Chocolate Milk Has Been Called 'The Best Post-Workout Drink,'" *Shape*, https://www.shape.com/healthy-eating/diet-tips/chocolate-milk-after-workout.

29. Allen Terrell, "But Was She Really the 'Witch of Wall Street,'" *Inside Adams* (blog), Library of Congress, March 14, 2012, https://blogs.loc.gov/inside_adams/2012/03/but-was-she-really-the-witch-of-wall-street/.

30. Stacy Horn, "Singing Changes Your Brain," *Time*, August 16, 2013, http://ideas.time.com/2013/08/16/singing-changes-your-brain/.

31. "Why Does Singing Make Us Happy?" *ShareCare*, https://www.sharecare.com/health/happiness/why-does-singing-make-happy.

32. Betty A. Bailey and Jane W. Davidson, "Effects of Group Singing and Performance for Marginalized and Middle-Class Singers," July 1, 2005, Sage Journals, https://journals.sagepub.com/doi/abs/10.1177/0305735605053734.

33. Stacy Horn, "Singing Changes Your Brain," *Time*, August 16, 2013, http://ideas.time.com/2013/08/16/singing-changes-your-brain/.

34. International Institute for Strategic Studies, *The Military Balance 2018* (London: Routledge, 2018), 192, 249–50, 422.

About the Author

Mary A. Kassian is a Word Guild award-winning author and international speaker. She has published several books and Bible studies, including *Girls Gone Wise, Conversation Peace*, and *True Woman 101*. Mary is a popular conference speaker at women's events such as *Revive* and *True Woman*. She has appeared on numerous radio and television shows such as *Focus on the Family* and *Life Today*. She has also taught cluster courses at Southern Seminary in Louisville, Kentucky, where she was recognized as distinguished professor of women's studies. Mary and her family reside in Edmonton, Alberta, Canada.